Destiny Re-Do

Turning Failure into Freedom
and
Planning into Perfection
A Guide by Skip Press

Destiny Re-Do

Skip Press

Published by Skip Press, 2024.

While every precaution has been taken in the preparation of this book, the publisher assumes no responsibility for errors or omissions, or for damages resulting from the use of the information contained herein.

DESTINY RE-DO

First edition. April 16, 2024.

Copyright © 2024 Skip Press.

ISBN: 979-8218990787

Written by Skip Press.

To everyone who ever wanted to go back and change their past. With this book, you can go back and change the *bad effects* or missteps of your past.

Dedication

To Rev. Bill McDonald, who taught me that
the power of love can conquer any mountain.

Introduction

This small book originated in an article I titled *How to Repair a UFO*. I thought that name would generate a chuckle or two and maybe some clicks on the Web. It did that, but because I have had so much personal success using the formula I describe herein, I expanded the story considerably.

I realized I needed much more than an article to explain this tool I'd put into effective use. My thinking needed a redo – maybe you can relate. And since the process was all about changing a situation in life for the better – a situation being *a destiny arrived at* – why not *Destiny Re-Do*?

This made more sense because most people I know think of destiny as unchangeable. You arrive and you feel you can't change the past. Perhaps you believe it was pre-destined and therefore immune to the exercise of your free will.

I've survived too many harsh situations in my life to give up in defeat when a new challenge arrives, no matter how dire it seems at any given moment. From many decades of experience, I know that destiny is malleable, fate is not permanent, and now I've narrowed down a way to improve my situations at any given point in life by mapping out how I arrived there and gaining understanding of the full journey.

To accomplish this, I developed a self-counseling tool that felt like it was dropped out of the cosmos like a gift. Accordingly, I initially described it as The UFO Experience. Why? Because I found the process magically, even other-worldly, effective. When I considered what the process repeatedly did for me, I realized it would start with an

–

Unintended Failure Occurrence

And when I finished, I felt I had an –
Unlimited Freedom Opportunity

I wrote the *UFO* article after solving two nagging personal situations by using a mental management technique derived by back engineering a famous phrase that some people attribute to the author of the legendary spiritual book *Tao Te Ching*. Supposedly, Chinese philosopher Lao Tzu said this:

> "Watch your thoughts, they become your words; watch your words, they become your actions; watch your actions, they become your habits; watch your habits, they become your character; watch your character, it becomes your destiny."

Perhaps Lao Tzu was credited because the *Tao*, published in 506 B.C.E., had progressions of logic in some of its 81 brief chapters that resembled the structure of the quote.

For example, this section from the twelfth chapter:

> Sight obscures.
> Noise deafens.
>
> Desire messes with your heart.
> The world messes with your mind.
>
> A Master watches the world
>
> but keeps focused on what's real.

Speculation aside, the quote first mentioned above, the one on which my formula hinges, has never been found in the writings of Lao Tzu. It has, however, also been attributed over the years to other famous persons including Siddhartha Gautama (the Buddha), Mahatma Gandhi, and British Prime Minister Margaret Thatcher. None of them authored it.

On his website *Quote Investigator,* Garson O'Toole revealed he found numerous possibilities including a version attributed to Frank Outlaw, President of the Bi-Lo supermarket chain, published in a Texas newspaper in 1977. That one read like this:

> Watch your thoughts, they become words;
> watch your words, they become actions;
> watch your actions, they become habits;
> watch your habits, they become character;
> watch your character, for it becomes your destiny.

I'd heard that one before, maybe even read it in a Texas newspaper when it came out, because I grew up in the Lone Star State and was an avid newspaper reader as well as having a newspaper route as a boy (the *Dallas Times-Herald*).

It doesn't matter where the phrase originated. It rang true to me, and I'm always on the lookout for useful truth. I was reminded of it while helping a client publish and promote a book he'd written. In one chapter, he mentioned an almost identical phrase to the Outlaw version. My client's book was about getting into a very tough situation – prison – and then getting out of it (conviction overturned on appeal).

As I contemplated the phrase in relation to my client's story, it occurred to me that I could reverse engineer the steps of the phrase and unravel the elements that led to his trouble. That's because I knew that, somewhere along the chain of events from thought to destiny, he had miscalculated his dealings with some people in government.

This wasn't speculation on my part – I knew the full story of how he ended up in prison, even his life story for that matter. So, I plotted out his sequence of events, and then I thought through the steps backward to when he won his appeal.

After that, I wondered if applying the formula backward would apply to situations in my own life, and I began to experiment.

Regarding the last step of the phrase, I chose to use Fate as the end result to work backward from, instead of Destiny. The idea of destiny suggests something lifelong, while a single situation can more easily be seen as a singular occurrence. Destiny can be viewed as God-willed, while most people I know have an inkling they can overcome misfortune with enough willpower.

In my life I've learned that, most often, my own actions led to any given situation, even if at first glance it seems it did not happen that way. Therefore, by honestly examining the sequence of events and taking full responsibility for each step, I reasoned I could develop understanding, and then, relief.

It's like getting the proper diagnosis by a doctor – with that, healing can often occur much more quickly. To me, the reverse engineering I envisioned was a "lightbulb moment" – a flash or insight or understanding, like a light turning on in my mind.

When ancient Greek scholar Archimedes stepped into a bath and saw the water level rise, he realized the volume of water displaced was equal to the volume of the part of his body that was submerged. This is now known as Archimedes' principle. He exclaimed *"Heúrēka!"* (meaning "I have found (it)!" That's how I felt about the idea of reverse engineering the phrase.

I began by examining Fate (the situation), then Character (what I was like at the moment I began thinking about the situation). As I examined any particular situation, the assumption was that my character was what brought me to the fate I was experiencing.

The next step of the process was Habits. Was there a pattern that I needed to change?

I then examined the Actions that began a habit pattern or placed me in the less than optimum situation. If it was a singular Action that led to the unfortunate circumstance, or repeated actions that became a pattern, I looked for the Thought or Thoughts that got the bad vibes giant snowball rolling down on top of me.

I used this technique on separate occasions to deal with things like money worries and an at times recurring feeling that people didn't like something about me but weren't saying what. (And I don't mean bad manners, bad breath, or body odor.)

Once I'd used the formula with uniform good results enough times, I wrote about the successful resolution of dealing with money worries in a Substack that I had been writing for over a year.

I have had a bit of a seeker's background all my life. Accordingly, I had examined many techniques that complimented and aligned with my new technique.

For example, I'm a big fan of the late great Shaolin monk and healer, Kam Yuen. I used his Yuen Method after seeing him lecture and then reading his first book. In dealing with a problem presented to me, it would always track back to a time and place in an adverse situation where the affected person felt helpless. It worked that way with me and, when using the Yuen Method with others, I repeatedly heard this phrase from people: "I felt like there was nothing I could do."

Since I mostly used the Yuen Method after ample time had passed since the initial incident, it was possible for me to remain "exterior" to the unfortunate situation being handled and bring about an understanding. This is reminiscent of the old axiom that others know what is wrong with you before you do, because they are outside looking in.

When working the Yuen Method with others, their subconscious resistance to fully confronting the situation was overcome with me there as a trained guide. In case you've never experienced hypnotism, it works the same way with a hypnotist as a guide, but the Yuen Method is not hypnotism at all.

The Yuen Method worked so well I once got someone's cold to go away while simply talking to them on the phone.

Which brings us back to the Fate part of my technique — where people think there is nothing they can do about any given situation.

Even if it's only a temporary feeling, they feel stuck. And when they adopt the "can't do anything" apathy, they mentally disempower themselves with regard to similar situations going forward.

My Destiny Re-Do technique is not something I use only to solve problems. When you fully understand the steps of the process, you can more easily map out a route to achieving any goal you come up with. Want to start your own business? That's a thought, so how do you describe it – what words? Then what successful actions do you need to take and which ones should you do habitually? Once you've worked all that out, you'll have the persona (character) necessary to achieve your goal – a fate you'll like, a destiny you've worked out for yourself.

You can achieve a Destiny Re-Do by back tracking, and a do-it-right destiny by planning out the logical application of the six steps I describe in this book.

This double whammy application of my method is why I've written this book – to enable anyone to try it out and hopefully get the kind of results I get on a regular basis. It doesn't involve psychic powers, hypnosis, religion, or any type of New Age woo-woo. It's just step by step to satisfying personal improvement.

Be patient in studying it and putting it into practice. If you have any questions or problems, I'm easy to find via my website at www.skippress.com[1]. I think you'll like what you're about to read, and I'd be happy to hear from you.

Skip Press

April 2024

---

1.   http://www.skippress.com

Step One:
What Was I Thinking?

IN MY EXPERIENCE, PEOPLE deal with three types of thought:

a. Emotion

a. Intellect

a. Intuition

One year, I gave a lecture at Pepperdine University in Malibu, California. My half-hour talk was about the story structure I developed and taught in my book *The Complete Idiot's Guide to Screenwriting*. I adapted the first edition of the book – which was later translated into Russian – into an online screenwriting course that was eventually available in 1,500 schools, colleges, and universities for almost 10 years.

The lecture is called *Skip Press on Screenwriting and the Hero's Journey and Elliott Wave in the Arts and Sciences*. You can view it at this YouTube link[2].

In Hollywood, movies start with an idea. Maybe the idea is to buy the rights to a successful novel and adapt it into a film or TV show. Perhaps someone writes an original screenplay with a clever story, and the script is eagerly bid on by producers. Maybe it's an idea to make a movie similar to another box office success. That's why, after the success of *Die Hard* starring Bruce Willis (1988) we got "Die Hard on a ship" which was *Under Siege* starring Steven Seagal (1992). There were other similar *Die Hard* imitations.

Ideas – thoughts put into action – can be highly profitable. Consider all the soft drink concoctions that started with an idea.

---

2.   https://www.youtube.com/watch?v=C5QE5ISZ_2o&t=729s

Coca-Cola was originally a drink with flavors of the African kola nut (caffeine) and the cocaine leaf (stimulant). The drink changed drastically over the years and had an altered destiny. John Pemberton, the original creator of Coca-Cola, had a medical degree. Addicted to morphine, he created his original drink as a substitute for the drug. By the time the drink was first bottled in 1899 in Chattanooga, Tennessee, Pemberton ownership was long gone as was the cocaine content of the drink. Cola syrup had originally been concocted to soothe an upset stomach, but it became a popular refreshment. By the time the first cans of Coke appeared in 1955, the drink was a national icon known and consumed all over the world.

Let's examine John Pemberton's possible thoughts that might have started him on Coca-Cola's destiny road. Which of the three thought categories above does it fit? Pemberton had an intellectual idea to create a morphine substitute. Since he was addicted to the drug after being wounded in the American Civil War, we may assume a substitute was a bit of an emotional idea as well. However, he owned a drugstore in Columbus, Georgia called Pemberton's Eagle Drug and Chemical House, and had a product known as Pemberton's French Wine Coca nerve tonic. So, it's more likely his primary thoughts in creating Coca-Cola were intellectual.

I'm not planning on inventing a new soft drink, and I have no addictions, so as I describe a thought to fate story from my own life, let's put aside intellectual and emotional and take up an intuitional thought that occurred one day when I was about seven years old.

My family lived in the small Texas town of Palmer, which was a partial setting for the movie "Tender Mercies." One autumn day, I was walking home from my girlfriend Diane's house and was about to cross the street when I stopped to admire falling leaves swirling magically in the wind. I already thought Palmer would be my whole life hometown and I was generally a very happy kid but then, seeing the leaves dancing before my eyes. I felt a distinct sense of spiritual peace and contentment. I thought, "This will be a remarkable life."

At that very moment, I was destined to be a writer. I began mentally chronicling all people and moments and things in my life that I considered important or at least memorable. Perhaps everyone does something similar, but I had a feeling I would be telling many stories in times to come, and I was gathering memories for later use.

Maybe my memory-gathering was not specifically geared toward future story material, but once I became a professional writer, I realized that's one thing I did in life, and where it started out.

That intuitional thought worked out well, although it was two decades before I began making money as a writer. After my first sale, I edited a Hollywood entertainment magazine and two others, produced and directed well-reviewed plays, sold screenplays and teleplays, sold hundreds of articles, was a staff writer for a network kids show and other shows, published novels and non–fiction books, and for almost a decade I taught that online course from my screenwriting book that was available in 1,500 schools.

There are over 40 books published with my name on the cover and dozens more that I either edited or ghost-wrote. Many won awards, and some hit #1 in their category on Amazon.

Prior to writing this book, though, I was concerned about what seemed like a bit of a career standstill, so I used my Destiny Re-Do formula and sorted something out. I had no idea if it would make a big change in my life, but I certainly felt better about my situation and was much more confident going forward. Then something amazing happened.

While posting on Facebook, I came across an ad and pursued it. Without listing out the details, I'll just say that within a week, I had a $30,000 deposit in my bank that I'm certain would not have happened if I had not used my formula and then seen that ad.

A couple of weeks later, while trying to figure out why I – like many writers and self-employed people – have had "boom or bust" times in my life that largely determined whether or not I had suitable housing. I used my formula once again and it backtracked to a time two years after my "interesting life" thought in Palmer, Texas. My envisioned future life in that town was upset when my father lost his job. My mother had four young boys and no outside job, and we ended up living in an abandoned shack in the country until rescued by relatives.

At the age of nine, I was too young to be able to do anything to help our circumstances. My *thoughts* expressed in *words* to my parents didn't lead to positive *actions*, and I got into a *habit* of being at the whim of others regarding living conditions. I grew accustomed to taking the best I could get. That *characteristic* caused me *fateful* problems in life, even as an adult.

So, after using my formula, I realized that not planning ahead and being proactive about an ideal place to live as an adult had been my downfall during good times. I resolved once more to write out my ideal living situation and be proactive and vigilant and never again have the thought that I couldn't do anything to improve my circumstances. In short, I had developed a long-term subconscious apathetic conviction that worked against my desires.

When I was married, my wife and I could never figure out where we wanted to live, ideally. Oddly enough, that had contributed to the demise of the marriage, and I'd been indecisive for years after the divorce about where I wanted my permanent residence to be.

After I used the formula about housing, I felt finally positive about my ability to work out a new place to live that I would love, one that all my friends and loved ones would enjoy. I had peace of mind about it all, which may sound trivial, but it was a great relief to me.

As you might imagine, my thoughts when living in the isolated shack in the country were very emotional. Circumstances got so bad that we ended up having nothing but white bread and margarine sandwiches to eat, with one glass of milk each day, and then we had no more milk. That's when the relatives arrived to move us to a better place, several counties away.

This echoes the Yuen Method results that I mentioned earlier, hearing from people I helped who felt powerless and had a thought that crippled their mentality about certain situations going forward, not realizing the mechanism they had put in place mentally. In our country shack in Texas as a young boy I, too, "felt like there was nothing I could do."

The thing is, though, I remember praying for help more than once. Maybe my mother overheard me and then walked to that farmer's house up the road. She asked to use the telephone and called my grandfather and uncles, and they came to the rescue. What moved her to do that was never explained to me, but I certainly did pray out loud.

Prayer is words, thoughts that can be silently expressed or openly stated, but before we move on to words as the next step of the formula, here's a bit more about thoughts and emotions.

What type of emotions are people least likely to express in words? Most people I know have trouble speaking about heavy emotions like shame or guilt. That is why people seek singular audience for comfort, like with a pastor or priest or psychologist – or even a trusted friend – when something is weighing heavy on their mind.

Anger is a heavy emotion which sometimes has its place as motivation to rectify an undesirable situation, but if someone is regularly seen as an angry person, they will often be avoided. Heavy emotional situations like that can make things even heavier mentally.

The emotions we most likely respond to favorably are lighter ones like joy, love, and peace. A baby's smile or laugh can move a parent to want to do everything they can to give their child a great life. Similarly, people in love will go to great lengths to express their thoughts. Romeo's glowing evening speech to Juliet in Shakespeare's play is an example. When a leader moves crowds with messages of peace, like

Mahatma Gandhi did, amazing things can happen. He was able to free his country, India, from British rule.

The lesson here is, when contemplating a situation, if you have a thought that prompts you to words and results in action, ask yourself if it's an emotional thought. If so, is it a positive, light emotion, or is it a heavy emotion like revenge, which is likely to have a bad result.

These days, with life coaches and all kinds of "positive thinking" gurus on the Internet and television, the general consensus is that light emotions have the greatest impact.

Many advisors, like Joe Dispenza, will tell you that, once you've planned a goal, you should function in life as though you've already achieved it, and God or "the universe" will bring your envisioned reality to pass. They're basically saying you should maintain personal certainty about the achievement of your goal, and in my experience that does work. I had a thought I would live an interesting life and another that I would be a writer, and despite many obstacles (such almost everyone in my family being against the idea of my chosen occupation), I made it.

Even in our sad family circumstances in the country shack, I was able to maintain an attitude that life would improve. I formed a mentality of trying to survive one day at a time. When I saw my younger brothers anguish about our circumstances, I drew pictures for them on lined school paper, or made up stories for them, or took them on adventure hikes in deep culverts near the house. I felt grief and apathy at times, but I never gave up, as illustrated by my prayers.

I did go through the five stages of grief: denial, anger, bargaining, depression, and acceptance as a nine-year-old country boy, but I didn't completely lose faith.

Intellectual thoughts pursued seem relatively simple to understand. I've found that meditation helps bring about a state conducive to better thinking and planning. When I say meditation, that could be as simple as a long hike. Thomas Jefferson reportedly walked five miles a day, and he did well enough. Even time spent in contemplation on a front porch or another comfortable place at the end of the day aids in excellent decisions. A walk on the beach can affect wonders; just ask most women who write online dating profiles.

As we grow older, we continually learn that thoughts are one thing, but research and testing of ideas are very important. This is why there are so many research and study groups out there. In the wealthy environs of Silicon Valley, *data is king*. Basically, the attitude is okay, good idea, but let's examine it.

Which brings us to intuitive thought. How do we deal with that? Are some people simply lucky guessers, or can intuition be nurtured and trained? The "remote viewers" of the famous Stanford Research Institute, which inspired the movie "The Men Who Stare at Goats" had proven innate psychic abilities. I met some of those people – Ingo Swann, Hal Puthoff, Ed May – and I also had the good fortune of knowing the late Alan Vaughan, who picked my resume out of a pile of 250 sent in from a *Los Angeles Times* ad. His friend Joe Brown was overwhelmed and didn't know where to start picking a ghostwriter. Alan handed him my resume and said "Hire this guy. He'll do a good job."

The book I wrote for Joe went to #1 in its category on Amazon.

I regularly use my intuition on scratch-off cards and my Instagram is filled with notices of wins of various amounts. The most I've won is $1000 – first $10, then $100, then $1000 – all within about 15 minutes, three scratch-offs in succession. I play the scratchers to practice my intuition, convinced that one day I'll be a multi-millionaire from the lottery.

If you can find a copy, I highly recommend Alan Vaughan's 1982 book *The Edge of Tomorrow* where he describes how he went from being a skeptical journalist investigating psychic abilities to an internationally recognized psychic who predicted the assassination of

Robert F. Kennedy, the Watergate scandal, and the Challenger space shuttle disaster.

According to neuroscientist and psychologist Joel Pearson, author of *Intuition: Unlock Your Brain's Potential to Build Real Intuition and Make Better Decisions*, the "superpower" of intuition is "the learned, positive use of unconscious information for better decisions or actions." He's correct, and I keep learning about it and using it positively.

While reading the book *The God Effect* about quantum entanglement, I learned that light is a combination of an electrical wave and a magnetic wave. That seemed to me to illustrate how some people associate more with the intellectual approach to life while others are more emotionally orientated. In storytelling terms, I equate the electrical wave to intellect, and the magnetic wave to emotion.

When movie and music stars are described, they're often called magnetic, and a great many of them make a living based on emotion. In contrast, we generally think of scientists and business people as having a more intellectual approach to life.

Truthfully, life needs both intellect and emotion, just as electrical and magnetic waves must be in balance for us to have light. So, while many see men as more "logical" and women as more "emotional" the truth is, we need both to keep the human race alive.

Do the sexes operate differently with intuition? I read once that the idea of "trust your gut" applied more to men, while empathic accuracy in women had more to do with "trust your heart." If so, that might align with the idea of a chakra, the Sanskrit word for an energy center in the body. According to this Indian science, the Manipura chakra located in the solar plexus area concerns confidence, self-esteem, and helping you feel in control of your life. In contrast, the Anahata chakra in the heart area is about the ability to love and show compassion.

Naturally, I've known both men and women who demonstrated an intuition concentration at both areas of the body. So, where are your thoughts coming from? Your stomach, your heart, of your brain? Or is it possible a thought could come from all three places at the same time?

I'll let you sort that out for yourself. Regarding watching our thoughts, I admire the words of Marcus Aurelius, a Roman emperor who believed Christian prayer saved his thirsty army when "water poured from heaven" and he and his troops immediately "recognized the presence of God." After that, he requested the Roman Senate stop early Christian persecution.

This author of the famous self-improvement book *Meditations* once said: "Our life is what our thoughts make it."

Thoughts are powerful, sometimes more than we realize, so it does pay to watch them very closely. I also watch what kind of thoughts I'm starting off with in any major endeavor, and if the thoughts I'm having are most appropriate in pursuit of my envisioned end goal.

And with that thought, let's go on to the next great aspect of my formula – *words*.

Step Two:
Words to Watch and Why

JOHN 1:1 OF THE KING James Bible says: *In the beginning was the Word, and the Word was with God, and the Word was God.* What does that mean? Well, in the original Greek text "the Word" is Logos, the creator of everything. So basically, it means there was nothing until God spoke.

When any of us has a thought and puts it into words, we're probably not intent on creating a world. We're likely expressing a thought that comments on the present, reflects on the past, or portends a future. We are creators of verbalized and written content. Each word's a creation, and the more precise we are with our words when we plan, the greater likelihood optimum action will proceed from our planning. The Law of Attraction that has gained such a following in recent years has a lot to do with stating goals precisely.

Across philosophies, the divine has different names, but the consensus is that it can only be understood by contact. It's like the idea of "Know before you go." Use the proper words to delineate your thought and you can be more easily understood. You can think of God, speak of God, but contact with God is an action; people pray and chant to get there.

Part of the process of growing up is learning to be more precise in description. Kids build their vocabulary as they go. That can be frustrating, but when you reach a substantial level of literacy and eloquence, it has great benefit. As a writer, I've often had people read something I wrote and then tell me: "I see what you mean, now that you put it that way."

Maybe you've tried to express something, been unable to think of the right word or phrase, and said "It will come to me" and then it did?

That kind of non-action with faith is often rewarded. You're expressing a trust in yourself to succeed. And you've exercised a universal principle.

In Lao Tzu's *Tao the Ching*, a passage says: "The Tao invariably takes no action, and yet there is nothing left undone." In Chinese, *wu wei* is the phrase for non-action but the principle is action through inaction. It's about not trying to force things and allowing some space for good things to happen. Some people feel the most effective prayers are said with full expectation of receipt and no further action, trusting we will be answered. Action through inaction, once prayed.

The Tao is about understanding the flow of things in the world in order to do best. Contemplation and meditation can reveal previously unseen realities. Verse Four of the *Tao the Ching* begins "The Tao is like a well: used but never used up. It is like the eternal void: filled with infinite possibilities."

What's my point? You choose your words, you state your case, and you have faith that your words will become validated with the achievement of your goal.

I once knew a famous actor, Ben Johnson, a pal of John Wayne who won an Oscar for his role in one of my favorite movies of all-time, "The Last Picture Show." Ben would never get upset about slow times. His philosophy was to "just sit a spell and something will come along." He raised horses when not acting and had a ranch in Arizona. Our mutual friend who introduced us told me a lot about Ben and how "sitting a spell" on a front porch with Ben was a memorable, meditative experience to be treasured.

In my own life, I once found great relief in life when I realized I had a pattern of things working out even in times when I felt I was facing fiscal doom. After my realization, I quit worrying and had trust in God, which was probably the reason things worked out, anyway. I've always felt God had a plan for me. Even if I didn't know the next step, I had faith.

If you're wondering why I'm dwelling on such things, it's that in using my formula to backtrack and unravel unfortunate life situations, I've found that trouble often hinges on something I've said after an erroneous thought I acted upon. Such as, opening my big mouth and choosing a partner out of loneliness and desire rather than first contemplating potential outcomes. I've continually learned great lessons after the most troublesome mistakes.

Why do words have such power? It's a fact that when you write out a plan or even an affirmation and repeatedly recite it, it's easier to make things happen. There is a famous children's book, *The Little Engine That Could* by Watty Piper. First published in 1930, it's about the under-sized Little Blue Engine who manages to pull a train full of presents to children waiting expectantly on the other side of a mountain. Every time the engine thinks she can't make it, she chants "I think I can, I think I can!" and she gets there and makes the kids happy.

This kind of exercising of the will, bolstered by words, has ancient roots. Consider the most popular word among practitioners of yoga and Eastern philosophies. "Om" is in reality not a word, however. In Hindu philosophy, it is an acronym and sound, out of which the universe was created. The pronunciation is "AUM" and each letter represents a Hindu god and a concept.

A – Brahma (creation or *satva* - goodness),

U – Vishnu (preservation or *rajas* - passion)

M – Shiva (annihilation or tamas - ignorance).

The letters are pronounced as follows: **A** (as in 'ah'), **U** (like the *o* in 'boot') and **M** (as the *m* in 'dam'). Many people chanting Om miss the **soft a** sound and think the word is just a **long O** followed by an **M**. Why is this important?

The ancient Upanishads say that from those three sounds all others are made. All that is past, present, or future is AUM. Whether you accept that or not, here's a scientific reality. When AUM is chanted, that's a vibration at the frequency of 432 Hertz (Hz), the same vibrational frequency found throughout everything in nature. You can hear this frequency on many recordings freely available on YouTube. Despite how ancient and natural the 432 Hz vibration may be, however, people mess with it.

Beginning in the 18th century, the A above middle C (known as A4) was the tuning standard for Western music. However, in different parts of the world, A4 in orchestras could range between 400Hz and 480Hz. Hertz is a measurement of frequency named after Heinrich Rudolf Hertz. He was the first person to prove electromagnetic waves exist. Remember what I said earlier about the composition of those waves?

With the use of different A4s in different places, conflicts arose. 432Hz was used by famous Italian composer Giuseppe Verdi and known as the Verdi Tuning, but not everyone used it, and attempts at standardization continued during his lifetime and afterward. In 1939, an international conference recommended that A4 be tuned to 440 Hz, now known as the "concert pitch" or the "Stuttgart pitch" and in 1955 this standard was adopted by the International Organization for Standardization.

In the 21st century, however, there is a growing belief, based on studies that have been done, that the use of 440Hz is detrimental to human health. 432Hz may indeed be more beneficial because music tuned from this frequency is easier on the ears, brighter and clearer, and contains more inherent dynamic range.

The most interesting thing is that 432Hz resonates with 7.83Hz (known as the "Schumann Resonance") which is proven to be the fundamental electromagnetic frequency of the Earth, often referred to as the planet's "heartbeat." This was discovered in 1952 by W.O. Schumann, a German physicist. He found that an electromagnetic energy wave revolving between the ionosphere and the Earth bumps into itself. The process amplifies frequencies and turns them into resonant waves.

You may be thinking, what does this have to do with the Destiny Re-Do formula? Well, isn't it interesting that chanting AUM harmonizes with Earth's heartbeat? Being in harmony with your environment makes you much more likely to make plans that succeed. Feeling in charge of your destiny because you know how to adjust it as needed is very empowering. A harmonious mentality is highly desirable, and my formula helps make it more possible.

The path from thought to destiny (or fate) can be corrected. When a musical vibration is not quite right, it can be out of tune, or not in harmony. You can write out a plan, but if it's not working out the way you want, it might need a rewrite. The right words lead to right results.

This discussion is all an example of how sounds formed into words have far greater impact than most people consider on a day-to-day basis. Have you ever had disturbing emotional thoughts about not having enough money, or food, or even a place to live? As I've described, I have – all of those. Maybe when I was younger, chanting AUM would have helped ease my situation, I don't know. What I do know is that sincere prayer helped, and I also know this – listening to excellent music has always smoothed my journeys. It was even more so when I became a father and learned of the magic of great classical music with babies and infants. Pachabel's Canon in D major, for example, is sheer magic. Find it at 432Hz on YouTube – you'll thank me.

The inspiration gurus say that worrying over what we do not have is a mentality of *"lack."* Much of their life coaching has to do with elevating one's vibration – mindset if you will – from lack to *abundance.* The first few times I used my process to improve things it had to do with feelings of *lack.* As I described, after one of the sessions using my formula, my mentality must have mightily altered my connection with the world, because a few days later my bank account multiplied by 15 times.

This is not to say I want to convince anyone to chant AUM or to have YouTube videos playing 432Hz sounds all day long. I'm simply pointing out how crucial the right words and vibrations can be in your life, and how concentrating on negative words and acting upon them can form lasting problems.

Now, let's get a bit deeper into sounds and vibrations, which is what all words are.

There is an emerging science that studies how sounds affect us, and in fact how they affect everything in life. It's called cymatics, derived from the Greek word "kyma" which means "wave." The name cymatics came from 18th century German physicist Ernst Chladni, who poured sand onto metal plates, rubbed a violin bow on the edge of the plate to vibrate it, and studied the resultant geometrical patterns that formed in the sand. It must have seemed like magic at the time because we cannot normally see sound. Since sound waves are slower than light, we see lightning before we hear thunder. Visual can seem to trump auditory but consider this. If you had to give up watching television or listening to music, which one would win?

Nikola Tesla said: "If you want to find the secrets of the universe, think in terms of energy, frequency, and vibration." Cymatics is all about that. It shows us that everything that seems solid is vibrating at its own rate, and those vibrations travel in waves.

Have you ever seen a resonance experiment where sand is poured onto an electrified metal plate and then a tone generator at various Hertz levels causes the sand particles to form different patterns? As the pitch of the tone increases, the beautiful geometric patterns formed in the sand become more and more complex.

Simple to complex is something I consider when writing. I try to tailor my text so that all kinds of people will understand it. When I first wrote young adult novels, I was told the average reading level in the United States was fifth grade. I hope it's still that high. The more I learn about the complex ways the universe works, the harder I concentrate to explain things in a manner easily understood by the most people possible.

Mark Twain once said that some people's writing was like fine wine while his was like water, and that a lot more people drank water. I've found when speaking to groups that it helps to assess the mindset of the group as best I can before delivering an address. To do that, I will ask some questions of people before I get started. Again, it's all about picking the right words for success, but I might also alter my tone to fit the audience. I know I'm getting through when I see pleased or relaxed looks or smiles Then I know I've found a comfortable resonance – or vibe, if you will – with my audience.

There is a scientific instrument called the CymaScope that makes sound visible. It allows the study of sound waves by imprinting sonic vibrations on the surface of ultra-pure water. Patterns of vibration on the surface of an object excited by sound is called "modal phenomena" and it's crucial in determining vibrational effects on everything from car parts to the human body. If you've ever wondered about healing via sound, the CymaScope helps in the study of that science. CymaScope.com has some fascinating links[3] about Sound Therapy and Music Healing. For example, each note of a piano forms a unique geometric shape that can be easily seen on the CymaScope. You can see the pictures on the company's website.

Years ago, I was fascinated by Dr. Masaru Emoto's book *Messages in Water*. He froze two different water samples. One was not spoken to before freezing, while the other was prayed over. Or love was expressed over another sample. When the ice from the "treated" samples were sliced and examined under a microscope, they resembled beautiful snowflakes. It made me think of examining snowflakes on my mittens as a kid, amazed at their beauty. Surely, they were the expression of God's love, falling from the heavens.

Austrian philosopher Rudolf Steiner said: "All of nature begins to whisper its secrets to us through sounds. Sounds that were previously

---

3.   https://cymascope.com/sound-therapy/

incomprehensible to our soul now become the meaningful language of nature."

Optimum thinking can produce better planning and the best words to describe the details. If you find yourself feeling shame or regret over circumstances, you likely can't get over the situation until you raise your mental vibration to a more contemplative and problem-solving state.

No sane person wants to be in pain or stay angry. Even ongoing boredom can be soul-killing. Letting these negative motions persist just attracts more of the same, so we need to elevate them.

If you force yourself to smile, you might find that your mood will lift. If you take your attention off your problems and start contemplating things for which you are grateful, you might get more things in life for which to be grateful. Maybe the song "Don't Worry, Be Happy" seems frivolous when you are in dire circumstances, but if you let your mind rest and be at peace, higher frequency emotions can surface.

It is popular these days – as it has been for generations – to use affirmations to create a mindset that attracts a lifestyle we desire. More than a mere wish, an affirmation is making a desire firm or even fixed in your mind. It's an assertion, a positive statement declared to be true. You are creating the world you desire with words. "I think I can, I think I can."

Do affirmations work? Well, there's a lot to be said about a maintained attitude. John Lennon reportedly said that when he was with The Beatles, as far as they were concerned, they were the best damn rock 'n roll group in the world, and that's why they were.

Maya Angelou said: "I am in charge of how I feel and today I am choosing happiness." She did pretty well, wouldn't you say?

Louise Hay said: "I choose to make the rest of my life the best of my life." She built a publishing house that inspired millions of people to live a better life.

Tony Robbins, whom I met long before he became the world's best-known success guru, said this: "The past does not equal the future unless you live there."

Affirmations are ancient in origin and practice. Consider these words from Epictetus, a Greek Stoic philosopher born into slavery who went on to establish a philosophical school. He said: "First say to yourself what you would be, and then do what you have to do."

Do what you have to do. This brings us to the next step of my formula – *action*. By now you may be wondering why I am describing the sequence of events in my formula going forward, when the technique is based on working backward from a fateful moment to unravel the roots of the problem. If you've asked that question, it's a good one. The answer is that a house might have a problem with a roof before anything else, but if its foundation is faulty, the house has a bigger chance of falling.

I am attempting to show you how any result is constructed, bit by bit, starting with the foundation of thought. As I stated earlier, you can use my formula in planning – becoming sure about a thought, choosing the right words to implement it, and choosing the best course of action. In my case, however, I had to fail with certain areas in my life and then disassemble the situations in reverse to understand how to not make the same mistakes again.

Whether in implementing speaking skills, writing skills, or simply choosing the right words to plan the best actions, it's important to see the full, big picture of any endeavor. That's why, in my first how-to writing book, the first chapter was called "The Big Picture." That book is called *How To Write What You Want & Sell What You Write*. It came from a class of the same name that I created and taught for UCLA Extension Writers Program, the largest of its kind in the world, taught only by professionals working in their field.

I sold that book to Career Press because I had an idea, based on my experiences with students pursuing various types of writing, that there wasn't a book like it and it would sell. I practiced a sales pitch, went to a big Book Expo in Los Angeles, and pitched what I just told you to the publisher. I got an immediate sale.

I have many examples in my life of honing an idea, working out the best words, and putting them into action to make a sale. So now, let's move on to the action step and I'll continue explaining how to sort out how the best courses of action can be determined and implemented in your life.

Step Three:
Taking Action in Heroic Fashion

EARLIER, I MENTIONED a lecture I gave at Pepperdine University in Malibu, California based on the story structure I developed and taught in my book *The Complete Idiot's Guide to Screenwriting*. That book came about from a talk I had with the author of another *Complete Idiot's Guide*. We were both speaking at a writer's conference in Dallas, Texas and she mentioned that the editors at alpha books (that's how they spelled it) were looking for someone to write a CIG on screenwriting. The book I was in Dallas to talk about was an edition of my *Writer's Guide to Hollywood Directors, Producers and Screenwriter's Agents*. Many writers wanted to know about that book because it was all about selling literary properties to film or TV.

My fellow author put me in touch with the acquiring editor at alpha books and I explained that although I had sold feature film screenplays, they had not been filmed. I had TV shows produced and was a staff writer on a network show, though. The company thought my background was good enough, and I got the job. I ended up doing three editions of the book before the company was acquired by a larger publisher.

A Russian firm, Triumph Publishing, surveyed all the other how-to screenwriting books and decided mine was the best, so they bought the rights. It is still selling in Russia as of this writing. The Canadian Writers Guild also did a study of the screenwriting books out there and named mine as the best for beginning screenwriters.

Even better, after legendary Hollywood agent Michael Ovitz left his job at Disney and started a management group, his company contacted me to turn my book into an online screenwriting course. Any school, college, or university that didn't have someone to teach screenwriting could have students sign up online and I taught them personally. I did that for almost ten years until the online education company was acquired by a much larger firm.

Getting the CIG Screenwriting contract is why I developed a story structure like but different than other story theories out there at the time. Before agreeing to write my book – concerned that not having a feature film made would be a detriment to my credibility – I studied all the other screenwriting how-to books and realized a great deal of pertinent information was missing. Hardly anyone discussed the influence of psychology in the movies. There wasn't much discussion about the most popular genres. I learned that very little had been written about the major influence women scenarists (the precursor to screenwriters) had in the early days of film, and also as filmmakers. I discovered that the most renowned female screenwriter of the 20th century, Frances Marion, was silent film superstar Mary Pickford's favorite wordsmith. I wrote about the early days of film and the influence of filmmakers about the world, like the Melies brothers in France and Sergei Eisensterin in Russia.

Including chapters about such things is one reason why my book was picked by the Russians and the Canadians, but I also knew I had to dig deep into what reliably worked in story structure to make a screenplay sell. I started by ranking sales by genre – vampire films were surprisingly far and away the winner – and then I expanded on the three-act structure.

This was a revelation. Aristotle's *Poetics*, a long essay written by the philosopher about plays of Greek playwrights, had long been a staple of story theory for writers. *Screenplay* by Syd Field was the reigning must-read book, one he'd written after working at a film company and reading hundreds of successful screenplays. He described a pattern that worked.

After the success of *Star Wars* and *The Road Warrior*, George Lucas and Dr. George Miller, the respective filmmakers, lauded the value of

Joseph Campbell's book *The Hero with a Thousand Faces*. This story structure was bolstered in Hollywood when Chris Vogler, working in story development at Disney, convinced executive Jeffrey Katzenberg of the worth of the Campbell work with a 14-page descriptive memo.

The problem I found was that the Campbell structure didn't work for all movies, not even if there was a very clear hero at the center of the story. I learned that when trying to come up with a "mentor" character (like Obi Wan Kenobi in *Star Wars*) in a romantic comedy I was writing.

If you don't know what Campbell's book is about, here's a short history. During the Great Depression, fresh out of college but unable to find a job, he spent five years studying world philosophies and religions and discovered a distinct pattern among many stories. Then he got a job teaching English at Sarah Lawrence University in Bronxville, New York. His discoveries formed the scope of the class he taught. One of his students had a publisher father, Campbell got a book contract, and that gave the world *The Hero with a Thousand Faces*.

I had long been a student of universal wisdom before writing my screenwriting book. Like Campbell, I studied everything I could about religions and philosophies. The more that I studied, the more I learned that great stories have much to do with the way things flow, the way things evolve in the world. Campbell isolated a story path that was parallel to many great lives as well as myths and religions.

For my *Writer's Guide to Hollywood* book I had interviewed Lew Hunter, co-chair of the screenwriting department at UCLA and author of the book *Screenwriting 434* (the name of his class at the school). Lew made the offhand remark that in the middle of the first act, you generally know what the movie is about. For some reason, that comment stuck with me.

I evaluated the structure of many movies I admired and movie heroes like Indiana Jones and Sam Spade, and I thought, these guys didn't have a mentor. In the middle of Act One of their films, however, you can figure out what the story is about. Stories could be about more than mere heroes. In *Cast Away*, the movie is about Time and how well you handle it. In *Chinatown*, the film is saying "Things are not what they seem." In the first *Star Wars* movies, the focus was on the villain, Darth Vader, but Luke learning about the Jedi (those who used "the Force") was the Shaping Force in my philosophy.

In the middle of Act One, I eventually concluded, the movie theme is revealed. I called that formation "the shaping force." It could be a hero, a villain, a concept such as Time, or even our choices in life and the values we hold, like George Bailey and the people of Bedford Falls in the classic film *It's a Wonderful Life*. Values that matter is the Shaping Force in that movie.

Great stories reveal themselves early and hint at what's to come. If you're a screenwriter, or even a novelist trying to sell your work, and you can't easily tell someone what the story's about, you're going to have a tough time. Your story might need simplification or at least another rewrite. As viewers, we pay close attention to figure out the gist of the tale. It pays to do the same in life, to win in new situations.

I have found that every individual life is *about* something; no one lives a meaningless existence. If you're lucky enough, you find out what it's all about early on and pursue a path that complements your instinct. The people who love what they do in making a living are said to "never work a day in their life."

Before I discovered my Destiny Re-Do formula, I found that I could plan out the progress in my life by aligning events with the transformational steps that take place within the Joseph Campbell matrix, and the heroic stories he discusses in his famous book. When I put together my own story structure encompassing other ideas, my new formula became an even better tool.

Here are the steps of my improved formula.

The Inciting Incident – This is a Hollywood term defining what gets the story started, an event that may seem to come out of nowhere.

Campbell called it "The Call to Adventure." Consider the arc of the Luke Skywalker character in the original *Star Wars* movie, which so many people have seen. Luke is living with his aunt and uncle, off to buy a useful robot, when his relatives are killed by evil forces.

The Shaping Force – As I explained, this term is mine. In the Campbell matrix this point in the middle of Act One is referred to as Supernatural Aid. That applies to Obi Wan Kenobi but the Shaping Force of the first *Star Wars* film is the spiritual development of Luke as he becomes a Jedi warrior. Obi Wan puts him on the path, but other elements aid in the transformation. In fact, the spiritual development theme carries through the entire *Star Wars* saga, wrapping up with *The Last Jedi*.

The Threshold – In Campbell terms, the hero (Luke) must pass Threshold Guardians to leave the planet he's on with the mentor he meets, Jedi master Obi Wan. At Mos Eisley, they escape the Old World of planet Tatooine and go to a whole New World which is the galaxy where a war is being fought by rebels against the ruling evil empire.

The New World – This is Act Two of a movie, often twice as long as either the first or third acts. The main character is learning the rules of the New World, struggling to master them and survive. In the first *Star Wars*, Luke is being mentored by Obi Wan. In another movie he's mentored by Yoda. He constantly faces, per Campbell, challenges and temptations.

Leap of Faith – In the middle of Act Two, there is a major test of what the hero or main character has learned. This usually involves overcoming a "wound" from the person's past; in Hero's Journey parlance it's called death and rebirth. I found in my own life that when I overcame some inner barrier that was holding me back, I could progress to a desired result. As an example, when I let go of trying to "force" meeting the right woman to marry and just trusted God and focused on my career, when I wasn't even looking I magically encountered the woman I later married.

There is a Campbell step between the middle of Act Two (my Leap of Faith) and the Return to the Old World, transformed. It's called *Atonement with Father* – where the hero must confront the ultimate opposing force in the story. Luke learns that the evil enforcer for the Empire, Darth Vader, is his father. It's a facing up to who you are and what you came from. I didn't pay much attention to this step when I formulated my structure. I assumed maturation would take place in the struggles in the New World, and the Leap of Faith mattered more than anything else.

The Deepest Dilemma – That's my term, a "How's he going to get out of this?" situation that seems like almost certain doom. Luke Skywalker flies into the Death Star. This, to me, is the most important step in the New World where the hero is tested and has to triumph to survive.

Return to the Old World – The hero or main character comes back transformed, having defeated the great threat to his place of origin and thus bringing back a "boon" to others. Luke blew up the *Death Star* and used his Jedi powers, which he continues to develop. The boon is the evil empire set back on its heels.

In my case, within six months of meeting the lady I'd longed for, we were married. I met her in New York, and she moved to California to live with me.

If you don't know the basics of storytelling but want to be a creative writer, you must learn them. You don't have to follow anyone's rules if you discover your own method that is embraced by others and gives you success. That said, here's what I incorporated into my structure beyond my Shaping Force.

I knew about three acts. Aligning Campbell's structure with three acts was already done by George Lucas and others. But what about William Shakespeare and his five acts? How did that fit into Hollywood storytelling? I didn't know for sure that he wrote plays with five acts in mind. Those acts were based on the timing of when the people at court wanted to take breaks. Many of Shakespeare's plays were performed at court when he was a member of the Lord Chamberlain's Men acting troupe.

My own story structure began to coalesce when I learned about the structure of light, and how it travels in waves. When I saw a picture of a wave of light taken by an electron microscope and its up and down oscillation, it reminded me of something I'd learned about the ups and downs of the stock market, of all things.

Huh? If you're scratching your head, I understand, but here's the explanation. A filmmaker I worked with told me about using the Elliott Wave theory to successfully play the stock market with techniques developed by R.N. Elliot in the early 20th century. Wildly enough, when I did some research, I learned that when I came to Los Angeles in the mid-1970s, I briefly lived in the house where Ralph Nelson Elliott was living when he came up with the Elliott Wave. My life has a lot of synchronicity.

Elliott's theory consisted of eight parts, and the "bull market" part was five "waves" of ups and downs. The "bear market" three waves after that was called a "recovery." I saw that the first up wave aligned with the progress from the Inciting Incident to my Shaping Force. Then it was a down wave to The Threshold to the New World. Why? Because the hero is always reluctant to leave the world he or she knows to depart to a new unknown world – that's a downer! Then another up wave, making uphill progress to the Leap of Faith, and when that leap is taken it's a downer to what I call the Deepest Dilemma where the world seems to say "Oh, you're all empowered now? Let's see what you've got!" (Like James Bond always getting captured by the villain.) And the final battle is an up wave and uphill battle to win. Goodbye, Death Star!

In review, my five steps (akin to Shakespeare's acts) were:

Inciting Incident to Shaping Force

Shaping Force to New World (Threshold)

Threshold to Leap of Faith

Leap of Faith to Deepest Dilemma

Deepest Dilemma to Conclusion and Return to Old World

This also aligned with the three-act structure. The first two steps were Act One. The next two steps were Act Two, and Deepest Dilemma to Conclusion and Return to Old World was Act Three (which could be quite short).

In the movie *Men in Black*, Act Three is only about eight minutes long. Tommy Lee Jones's character is swallowed by the giant alien bug (Deepest Dilemma). This in Campbell terms is The Belly of the Beast. With a weapon the big bug has swallowed, Jones blows a hole in the beast and escapes. It's a long action sequence. The result is the true test of all of the transformation that has taken place. And so, there's another example of why it's good to have both ups and downs. That's reflective of life, nature, and light itself.

The downer that I call the Deepest Dilemma is like, okay, you're so smart. Let's see what you can do. Then the hero marshals everything that's been learned, and boom, it's a big up at the end.

I compared my structure to many movies and found out it worked, over and over. It amazed me that even Shakespeare's *Hamlet* fit the pattern, as did *Cast Away*.

Early in 2024, I did an online three-day seminar with Tony Robbins, whom I met long ago before he ever gave a seminar. He was living in an apartment on Venice Beach, California at the time we met in the mid-1970s. I'd never read any of his books or taken one of his seminars before 2024, so I decided to check out his "Time to Rise" Summit. I was amazed to discover that Day Two was mostly about his interpretation of the Hero's Journey. I listened to what he had to say but I didn't learn a single new thing that day, because of all the study I'd done prior to hearing him. His seminars were largely what I expected, because when I met him he was going around trying to meet very successful people and find out their secrets of success. Years later,

I realized he was following the formula Napoleon Hill claimed to have followed before writing the book *Think and Grow Rich*.

Still, Robbins has motivated a lot of people and made a lot of money. From everything I can tell, his spiel mostly has to do with isolating patterns, adjusting them, and doing things that make you enthusiastic about life and living. Understanding flows and patterns is very important.

Lives have patterns that repeat. I ended up married in a pattern that distinctly followed the structure I discovered. Knowing that the pattern exists, the more I learned about it, the more I realized that I could figure out where I was in any endeavor, and then know roughly what might happen next, following the pattern. It was an action plan I could depend upon.

The reason that the Joseph Campbell book speaks to so many people is because he studied great lives, religions, and philosophies, and he found that there were repeating patterns. He wrote down his research and honed it while teaching before he authored his initial book.

I learned story structure, innovated it with my own discoveries, and found that I had a formula that worked not only in telling stories, but in living my life. Many times, I would start off with a singular idea, the inciting incident that started my journey. Like moving to Los Angeles to become a writer while also looking for a particular person to marry that by "normal" logic might deem impossible to find. Only, my love idea – the thought that started it all – was mirrored at my journey's end.

All along the way, my journey was fueled by unflagging faith. My determination wavered at times, but I never gave up. I hit several "I don't know if I can do this anymore" points but didn't quit. You know, "What doesn't kill you makes you stronger."

What kept me going? My Shaping Force. I had a thought to achieve a certain life and I kept putting it into words, making plans, changing a plan when warranted, and working every plan I came up with. Thoughts to words to actions!

My story structure, my flow of actions, encompasses ups and downs, the natural flow of life. Downs are okay, we learn from them. We hit resting points sometimes, and great stories mirror life's natural ride. That's why we like the journey, which enhances our dreams and emotions.

If you don't expect life to be always an upward trajectory, you'll probably have more energy. If you doubt the strength of your original idea, though, the energy necessary to achieve it will decrease. I saw people in Hollywood and elsewhere give up on dreams when they ran into opposition that they thought they could not overcome. They went into self-doubt and let the negative mentality win.

The people that I know who have succeeded in Hollywood and other high goal endeavors somehow never stop working on their goal. If they doubt the journey, they get over that. They might have their downs, but they always come back up.

Your original ambitious idea is usually the strongest because it generates the story and its details. For the most part, no one but you make the actions in your life happen. When I'm having trouble achieving something and I apply the Destiny Re-Do formula, it often comes back to my giving up on a goal – *stopping the action*. That can usually be rehabilitated, or a new and improved goal formed and pursued, so I reformulate and resume.

Like Joseph Campbell, I have studied universal wisdom all my life. One of the very best lessons about pursuing a goal I got from a page I found in the *Wall Street Journal* one day. It's a quote from Mencius, number three in popularity of philosophers in China after Lao Tzu and Confucius. He said this:

"Heaven, when it is about to place a great responsibility on a man, always first tests his resolution, wears out his sinews and bones with toil, exposes his body to starvation, subjects him to extreme poverty, frustrates his efforts so as to stimulate his mind, toughens his nature and makes good his deficiencies. Men for the most part can mend their ways only after they make mistakes. Only when they are frustrated in mind and in their deliberations can they stand up anew. Only when their intentions become visible on their countenances and audible in their voices can they be understood by others. As a rule, a state without law–abiding families and trustworthy Gentlemen on the one hand, and, on the other, without the threat of external aggression, will perish. Only then do we realize that anxiety and distress lead to life and that ease and comfort end in death." ~ *Mencius, Book VI Kao Tzu, Part II, 15*

Mencius lived 72–289 BC, and his book of the same name was written when women were the keepers of the home. So only Gentlemen are mentioned by him, but his principles apply to any sex, and the words are perfectly applicable in today's world.

When you have a great idea, maybe an original idea, or an entrepreneurial idea that might change the world for the better, or even one that simply makes life better in your community, you're going to run into opposition. You're going to have ups and downs, so get used to it. It's all the natural flow of life, the way life flows. Maintain your idea, don't doubt it, choose your words well, and have a voice that can be easily understood by others. They will assist you in your actions because they will see the benefit those actions will bring them.

On the other hand, you could just look for a comfortable life and something you can depend on. You could live a self-centered existence where you pursue luxury and ignore the plight of others. Or you could get depressed, give up and go into a downward spiral. Any of those situations will result from getting caught up in habits. We'll take that up next and see how habits can be either devastating, or dependably transforming.

Step Four:
How Habits Form Character

HABITS ARE GOOD AND habits are bad. Habits are horrible when you get into a persistent pattern that, even if you realize it is negatively affecting you, you don't know how to change. I rediscovered that just before it came time to start writing this chapter.

I've often experienced my world being in synch with what I'm working on at any given moment. This time, it manifested in my coming to a complete standstill with my writing.

I work hard, and Easter weekend was coming. I wanted to finish the book before that weekend. Unfortunately, I began feeling very down, living in my mountain home with winter still holding on. Another snowstorm! Would it ever end? Normally, I would have been okay, but now I couldn't bring myself to get anything done. I decided to just rest and reflect. I simply didn't feel mentally capable of doing much. Maybe I simply needed a break.

I forced myself to relax and reflect and finally, I recalled the first time in my life when I felt so down. When my mother married my stepfather the year I graduated high school, they opted to move to a larger town and a bigger house. I had three younger brothers and we shared bunk beds in a small bedroom in our tiny home. No man newly married would want a bedroom separated from the boys' room by only a door, however. It made sense for the adults to move, and I began intuiting that I didn't fit in with my mother and stepfather's plans going forward.

In the new house in the new town, my stepfather got me a job at a foundry. The economy wasn't very good at the time, and it seemed like the only job I could find. The air at the foundry was horrible. I would come home looking like a coal miner after work. It was hard to scrub all the soot off my skin that had seeped in under my jeans. My lungs weren't doing too well, either. Finally, I quit, and that gave my stepfather fuel to call me a slacker. Given his demeanor, I was his enemy.

Long story short, I ended up getting kicked out of the new place by my stepfather.

Stunned about this turn of events, I managed to rent a small room I could barely afford in a house nearby. Shortly thereafter that cold winter, I became deathly ill with the flu. All my friends now lived quite a way off. In my new place, with no energy to get out of bed, no telephone, really no one to call and ejected from my family, I thought perhaps I was going to die.

It was devastating because family had always meant everything to me. Too much, probably. I'd been protecting my brothers for years after our parents divorced and my father was not around much. It didn't seem to matter to my elders that I wanted to stay close to my brothers. The lack of empathy displayed by my mother when I was kicked out was also devastating. I hadn't done anything to deserve what happened.

Obviously, I made it in life because I'm here. I have had dozens of books published and cultivated an international readership. I've done alright for myself, but I wasn't thinking of that when I considered other times in winter when I'd been alone and felt isolated.

Then, as I reviewed the bad root incident in my mind, I realized I had a bad habit. As I plugged onward writing this new book, I'd done so while having indigestion all week. I was ill enough, I wondered if I had some disease.

After I recalled the original "bad incident" in my past, however, the trauma stored in my "second brain" (stomach) was released. The tummy problems vanished, and my energy and mood began elevating.

This kind of personal resurrection was not a new thing. I had much experience revitalizing my life in down situations like that. Now, I knew I'd handled something major with the resolution of what made me feel so darn *stopped*. Having studied the Yuen Method with legendary healer and Shaolin monk Kam Yuen, I knew from using it on myself and with others that once the primary problem was isolated and reviewed, healing could be very quick, or even instantaneous.

My negative **thoughts** about moving from my hometown were troubled. I voiced my objection (**words**), which angered the stepfather who was basically an insecure bully. At his own funeral, his children who never spoke to him (I never found out why) did not attend. So, my **actions** in not getting along with him became a **habit** that caused me a lot of grief at later times. The unexamined trauma of being thrown out of my family and getting very sick lurked in my subconscious, waiting to be triggered by similar circumstances.

That's an illustration of what a bad habit can manifest. How about the other side of it? What's the flip side of a bad habit? Thankfully, I'd been teaching about those for years. When I first taught screenwriting online, many of my students complained about not finding the time to write. To ease their concerns, I gave them an example of renowned screenwriter John Milius, who I'd been told wrote only two pages a day. With screenplays at the time being about 120 pages, that meant in two months a person would have a first draft script.

That suggestion helped a lot of aspiring screenwriters. I later found out from a friend who was a close friend of Milius and wrote a biography of him that John would write five pages a day, but I'm glad I told students two pages, because that was much easier a goal for them to confront.

Another suggestion I often made to writers of all kinds was about finding time to write. Work, relationships, kids, civic duties in their lives would clash with their ambition. Or, people they lived with wouldn't respect their space when they tried to write. (This is not uncommon with family and friends who never considered good writing to be something they could accomplish.) I told my correspondents to be very firm and make it clear to everyone, no exceptions, that unless it was an emergency, they should have at least an hour a day set aside, the same specific time, and not be interrupted. Once their friends and loved ones realized that was an inflexible schedule, my aspiring writer would be left alone, as if a memo had gone out to the universe.

I knew it would work because I'd used it successfully in my own life, even if I had to ruffle a few feathers to establish it. That was a good habit I'd seen work for everyone without exception.

So, what is a habit, anyway? It's something done repeatedly. When it's done consciously, such as a proven successful way of doing business, it can be great. You can get in the habit of winning at any chosen activity or profession. When you find yourself in a difficult struggle and lose at an endeavor *and* believe there is nothing you can do to change the situation, that can become a habit that may recur as you move forward in life.

Have you ever heard someone described as a loser? If it's a reputation based on actual experience, I am certain there is a pattern or at least a traumatic situation in that person's life that got the rumor started. Maybe they act like a loser now, but did they always?

Often, when I counseled people using the Yuen Method, they would reflect back to an incident where the whole trouble started, and they had decided there was nothing they could do about it. In fact, I repeatedly heard the same phrase from people who didn't know each other. They would say as if reading the same script: "I felt like there was nothing I could do." I've already explained that, but it bears repeating. I hold you can always do something – if not now, later.

What happens to a person psychologically at the surrender point? They subconsciously *turn off their personal power* regarding handling similar situations going forward. Kam Yuen would explain it in computer terms, the mental mechanism being like on/off switches in the mind. When I would counsel people using that method, usually long after the initial problem had occurred, they were no longer caught up in the activity and thus could look at the incident objectively.

Then they would either realize there was maybe something else they could have done way back when. At the least, they saw where it all started and that new mentality "flipped the power switch" back on and they were no longer subconsciously anchored. Thus, they were immune to being triggered in similar situations going forward.

I'm not a licensed psychologist or life coach, never try to be one, but I've been sharing things that have worked for me and others for years, so take that information as you will.

Someone I've learned a lot from, Paramhansa Yogananda, the founder of the Self-Realization Fellowship, said this about habits: "Every human activity, whether it be performed as an outward physical movement or as an inner process of thought, is a vote for a particular habit." He described habits as mental phonograph records where repetition of actions form subtle mental pathways in the brain. Each time the action is repeated, the pathways get deeper until the slightest attention "plays" the action. This can happen over and over.

We see this with professional people of all kinds, particularly with musicians and athletes. That NBA superstar you admire for astonishing success hitting three-point shots has spent years practicing the shot until "muscle memory" was formed in the brain, making the excellent action look automatic to an outside observer.

If you've ever seen a pro golfer at the top of his or her game, or if you've ever played the game well, I'm sure you know how visualization of a shot before it's executed can be very important. When I was in high school and our team won a state championship, I learned this lesson over and over. When my mind was caught up in emotion and not in visualizing my shot and following through, I didn't do nearly as well.

I edit books and rewrite scripts. People who are not yet pro writers are often amazed at how quickly I resolve story or dialogue problems, or get a project reworked. Writer's block? I've handled it many times. Maybe you could call my problem that I described earlier as a writer's block of sorts. I see it more simply. I've learned to keep digging until I find a solution.

The writing that I do often (usually every day) seems easy enough for me, but I have honed my words and other skills for decades. I have habits about how I approach different tasks, and I do indeed feel "subtle pathways" have been activated in my brain that affect my approach to work.

When you hit upon an impasse and use the formula I outline in this book to backtrack and solve the problem, it's likely you might make a potent discovery when you get back to habits. Having and/or displaying a certain character or personality can land you in a seemingly inevitable point of fate but remember – character is the result of habits. It can be changed.

Let's use a sports example, the basketball legend Michael Jordan. Not only does the National Basketball Association website state that "Michael Jordan is the greatest basketball player of all time," the NBA Most Valuable Player Award is the Michael Jordan Trophy. As a high school sophomore, however, he couldn't join the basketball varsity because at 5 feet 11 inches, he was too short for the team.

That didn't stop him. The next summer, he grew four inches, and after starring on the varsity, as a senior he was selected to play in the McDonald's All-American Game.

Playing for the University of North Carolina, he made the game-winning jump shot in the 1982 NCAA Championship game, and you probably know the rest about his stellar NBA career.

Is there any doubt that Michael Jordan developed playing habits and the attitude of a total winner to achieve the success he did? What if he had let not making the varsity as a sophomore traumatize him? Only, he didn't; he was such a star on the junior varsity he scored 40 points in some games.

Jordan was not without negative habits, however. In 1993, he admitted that he had to cover $57,000 in gambling losses in 1992. One man claimed he won over a million dollars from Jordan in a game of golf. When Jordan retired from the NBA the first time in 1993, there were rumors (never publicly proven) that the NBA wanted him retired due to gambling.

In 1994, he played professional baseball to fulfill a dream of his late father, who saw his son as a pro ballplayer. He went back to basketball the next year, though, and for the second time, he led the Chicago Bulls to a three-peat as NBA champions. Michael Jordan was such a habitual winner that Larry Bird, himself a legendary player with the Boston Celtics, described his rival this way: "God disguised as Michael Jordan."

I wouldn't compare my career to that of M.J. by any stretch, but there are parallels and contrasts. As a sophomore in high school, I became convinced I could make it as a writer when I read a short story of mine aloud in English class. Girls I admired oohed and aahed and after school the teacher tried to seduce me. (I hustled away from that one.) When I became a pro writer (my version of the "varsity" in media) my career kept climbing. When I added up some numbers a few years back, I realized that with my books and classes, I had helped half a million people become better at writing.

I never had a gambling problem like Jordan, but many times in my life, I would put family concerns above my own, to the point it caused resentment. It was a weakness that started when my mother divorced my father, and her brother Charlie (my uncle) made me promise to be "the man of the house" and look after my brothers like a surrogate father. My stepfather accepted them but didn't want me around. I felt I had to hold on to help them have a better life and I didn't trust him to help with that.

I never stopped trying to help my siblings. At some point, each of my brothers lived with me when we were adults, as I helped them get started in a new city where they all prospered. It was an ingrained habit for me to always look after their welfare.

Plotting my personal story against my formula, it was my uncle's **idea** and **words** (well-meant, no doubt) that I agreed to, prompting **actions** I considered a thoughtful father would do, that became a **habit** that made me at times seem an intrusive **character** to my brothers. Thus, the **fate** of troubled family relations at times.

I suppose I even had a gambling problem of sorts, like Jordan. I never got much of an education in fatherhood from my father, grandfather, and certainly not my stepfather. So, I gambled that my logic and wisdom I accumulated as I went along, as well as inherent Christian values, would prove correct when I tried to advise my siblings. Sometimes I was right; sometimes I was wrong. I was better at helping family after I became a father myself, but I was operating on my own thoughts of how to go about it, not following a promise I made to a caring uncle.

I hope you don't mind the self-examination I share here. The purpose is simply to illustrate the power the Destiny Re-Do formula. Starting with a well-considered positive thought, an inspiration perhaps put into words as a positive game plan, good actions can be pursued. When those positive actions are habitually and faithfully repeated, you form the character of a winner, and your desired destiny can be achieved.

Working backward from a step of overall destiny that I deem as fate, you can ask "What kind of character would end up in this place?"

Then, what kind of habits would form that character, and what actions form those habits.

You get the point, I'm sure.

And it all starts with a thought, or thoughts. Here's how powerful they can be. Nikola Tesla, who brought the world alternating current and many other benefits, said this about how he would think about an invention before trying to diagram it or create it:

"I do not rush into actual work. When I get an idea, I start at once building it up in my imagination. I change the construction, make improvements, and operate the device in my mind. It is absolutely immaterial to me whether I run my turbine in thought or test it in my shop. I even note if it is out of balance. There is no difference whatever, the results are the same. In this way I am able to rapidly develop and perfect a conception without touching anything."

Early on, I would thoroughly visualize stories in my mind before I would try to put them into words. Once, when writing the first book of a series of novels, I noticed that my characters were so well-envisioned and understood by me, I was at one point just "watching a movie" and typing out what I was seeing in my mind.

Now, in 2024, with the AI model Sora, anyone can "create realistic and imaginative scenes from text instructions." Only, there's a catch. The visual result is highly dependent upon how well and specifically detailed are the words you put into text.

And that takes some well-considered thought.

That said, we're getting closer to the finish line. What about character? Once that's established, aren't you rather locked into a certain fate?

Maybe yes, maybe no. Let's have a look.

Step Five:
From Character to Fate, Make It Great

WHAT IS DESIRABLE CHARACTER? I offer another sports example. The most famous coach in college basketball history is John Wooden. He not only built a championship empire at UCLA; he instilled great character in his players. He had many fine things to say about character, the most notable being this: "The true test of a man's character is what he does when no one is watching," Naturally, that goes for any gender.

Coach Wooden also advised: "Be more concerned with your character than your reputation, because your character is what you really are, while your reputation is merely what others think you are."

Who people think you are can have a lot to do with success, particularly if you are an entrepreneur or any kind of innovator. That's been true for ages. It can also have to do with failure when you think you're riding the wave of something wonderful. Galileo Galilei suffered from going against "settled science" when he supported the Nicolaus Copernicus proposal that the Earth revolved around the sun, rather than the other way around. To the Roman Inquisition in 1615, Galileo was crazy. In truth, he was right – it just took the world time to catch up.

Galileo said: "All truths are easy to understand once they are discovered; the point is to discover them." What he found out was that it can take the world an agonizing amount of time to discover you are correct in your assertions and actions.

You have likely heard the belief that everyone else knows what's wrong with you before you know. That might not always be true, but it's common enough. As I relayed in the last chapter, when viewing a situation from an outside perspective, removed from the time and place of an incident, clarity is much more possible.

Everyone has a point of view even if they're stuck in it; the bigger picture provides more data.

In astrology, there is a parallel. Perhaps most people in the world today know their "sun sign" determined by the month and date when they were born. Astrologers say it can determine how you look at life. Most astrologers will tell you, however, that what is more important is the "rising sign" which influences physical personality, physical appearance, and societal compatibility. That one influences how people perceive you, particularly at first meeting. The rising sign, also known as the ascendant, is calculated by the zodiac sign rising on the eastern horizon at the exact moment (date, hour, minute) that you were born.

You can think of your sun sign as your inner identity, while your rising sign is your outer identity (or "mask") that the world sees.

I'm not touting astrology, just illustrating how you can perceive yourself one way and be seen in an often very different light by others. That's the way of the world. It's why we have the phrase "getting to know you."

This is crucial when using the Destiny Re-Do formula. You may have reached a "fate" of sorts where in reality your character was above reproach, the habits you had in getting there were admirable, your actions were tireless and correct, you worked out excellent plans before taking action, and your initial thought was accurate.

Except, what if you're in a Galileo situation? People you have to deal with can upset your whole effort by wrongly deciding your character is flawed, as the Inquisition did with Galileo.

On a personal note, while musing over troubles I had with my stepfather as a young man, I considered the fact that it never occurred to me to tell my mother and stepfather that my Uncle Charlie (her brother) had made me promise to be the "man of the house" and look after my brothers. Had I done that, rather than not trusting this new man in our lives, my stepfather *might* have told me he would take over and do his best to help my brothers as they grew up. As it worked out, he did that, moving them to Alabama and building a house where they all lived up through high school.

My mother, who desperately needed a man in her life, barely able to make it economically, was willing to sacrifice me to keep her new arrangement in place. I ended up ejected from my family If I had told her what her brother made me promise, would it have made her more empathetic?

This is all speculation, but one *major thing* I do when I use the Re-Do formula is to take responsibility for my actions first, and not seek to assign responsibility for my destiny destinations to others. Typically, at any step in my life that I examine, I was doing the best I could with the knowledge and expertise I had at the time. Maybe I wasn't sometimes. That's not the most important element, though. What matters most is to simply find the truth and gain understanding, so that I can free myself from the lasting effects of erroneous detours and wrong turns of the past.

I discovered at a certain point in my life that I could not lie or cheat. I'm not trying to appear as a young George Washington who chopped down a cherry true and fessed up to it (a made-up story that never happened). I'm not attempting to present myself as having an "Honest Abe" Lincoln personality. The fact is, I've simply studied so much about religions and philosophies that, with a basic solid grounding in the ways of Jesus of Nazareth, I realized one day that when I thought of lying to someone, it would instantly affect me negatively. Why? Because I would be creating a false reality in my life and theirs.

Similarly, when calculating what a client owed me for services rendered, I thought about "rounding upward" the amount. I didn't do it, though, because I could see that act impacting my income going forward. That's how the idea of karma works – your actions fuel your fate.

This isn't to say you shouldn't use your wits to talk yourself out of a threatening situation when you are in danger. In a pinch, a "little white lie" might save your hide. I'm simply convinced by decades of experience that honesty is the best policy in almost all aspects of life.

Good people are their own harshest critic. With karma, you get back what you put out. It's the biblical "you reap what you sow." The word karma, derived from Sanskrit, means an action and the consequence that naturally follows. It's basically the same as Isaac Newton's third laws of motion of classical mechanics: "To every action there is always opposed an equal reaction: or the mutual actions of two bodies upon each other are always equal and directed to contrary parts."

That is generally stated as: "For every action there is an equal and opposite reaction."

Without getting too physics-ical, I'm sure you have similar examples in your life. Touch a hot stove, get burned. Trust the average politician, learn a lesson. Believe that Hollywood tells historical stories accurately, risk disappointment. The lesson is that it really does matter, per John Wooden, that you are the same when no one is watching as you are when everyone is watching.

I've often met people who were impressed by some famous person I have personal experience with. They'll tell me how nice that person was because of one simple meeting they had. I usually don't bother trying to educate them on someone unless they ask for my opinion. Or, if I know the person they're impressed with is a bad person they should avoid.

If you're honest with yourself, you inherently know who you are, and how you've been, at any given point of your life. People who know you well know that, too. When someone tells a friend of yours that they don't like you because of something you said or did, a likely response from a true friend might be something like: "Really? That doesn't sound like him (or her)."

It's wonderful to be of good character, but we must deal with public perception in almost every aspect of life. This is why public relations firms are paid high wages to manage reputation, even when they have to cover up despicable acts. How people truly feel, what they actually say both in public and behind the scenes, and what they do in the public and when no one is watching are all important factors, but it is folly to expect anyone to instantly "get" who we are or who anyone else is deep inside.

In marketing, guessing about people is rarely as valuable as raw data about their regular activities. That's why marketing firms want personnel who thoroughly understand Search Engine Optimization (SEO) principles.

Correct immediate assessment of who we are happens sometimes, but the 21st century has largely been about media manipulation of people and the exposure of that manipulation. Fakes and lies are exposed every second, with resultant uproar. Because of the ongoing evolution of perception in the world, people now seek actual truth probably more than ever in history.

It comes down to this. In today's world, it could be impossible to not have a reputation. In some societies like China, however, personal reputation is escalated to a horrible Orwellian degree. Using all-pervasive electronic surveillance, each Chinese citizen has a Social Credit Score that, if not meeting established communist standards, could mean a person cannot travel, get a job, or even buy food. Supposedly established to establish trustworthiness of people and institutions – which sounds good as an aim – their system is actually about adherence to control by the state. It is the antithesis of the American ideal of individual freedoms.

In contrast, people in the United States who learn how to game the system and cheat government programs meant to uplift the needy, such as welfare or medical benefits, make the idea of a social credit score look attractive. Which means crooks prosper and American society spirals downward, aided by politicians who get rich in office far beyond the expectations of the salary they receive from taxpayers.

Can legislation formed and passed by crooks not result in being gamed by the criminal element?

Admirable character is of utmost importance, but it cannot be legislated or ordered. It has to be learned and adhered to by each individual. When we hear phrases in life like "Who has the most toys, wins" and success is presented by the media as having a million-dollar home and a vehicle costing hundreds of thousands of dollars, the emphasis is only on public perception.

There is an old television news maxim that "If it bleeds, it leads." This means a fatal car wreck or major disaster gets the highest priority in a newscast. The problem is, it's like traffic slowing down to "lookee-loo" at an accident. Continued news emphasis on the worst events in life can make the world seem to be much more dangerous than it is.

When I grew up, there were only three major TV networks, and people mostly saw TV news early in the evening. If they wanted more comprehensive information about local events, they read the newspaper. Papers would have the more sensational news on the front page, but much more data was in the sections on sports, business, local events, and entertainment like comics and movie attractions.

I see a trend going on these days. I have millennial children, and they and generations younger than them have moved away from cable networks and the hundreds of channels available. They get their news from the Internet and the videos of YouTube and Tik-Tok. They have more input choices than ever before, yet the trend is away from "information" overload.

Character also counts more than ever. When it's hard to tell whether a video presents actual events or manipulated Computer Generated Images (CGI), you get an increasingly skeptical society. Artificial Intelligence (AI) makes it worse, image-wise. The Gemini

AI from Google proved that decisively in 2024 when people asked that images be created of American Founding Fathers, and they got a response depicting all the Founders as black.

Then, the person responsible for the Gemini algorithms at Google – a Caucasian man – said he make the AI that way on purpose. He was apparently trying to make some "woke" statement about American culture. While Google has created many useful things for the world with its search engine, email, business tools, and excellent visual maps of the Earth, this AI boondoggle was a major threat to its reputation as a company.

Since we all know we must deal with how others perceive our character, we can just do our best and leave it to fate how we're viewed or understood. That's not often the best way to live life, though. When planning out any course of action, it pays to consider potential public perception and try to find acceptance with as many people as possible.

Chinese philosopher Lao-Tzu was an advisor to an emperor, but he also wrote poetry. He didn't write it only for people at court. He also didn't keep it for himself like American poet Emily Dickinson. The legend is that he would test a new poem with the local flower lady and gauge her reaction. If she liked it, he felt most people might do so as well.

Perhaps the most widely quoted writer in history, William Shakespeare, had a similar attitude. His plays presented at the Rose and the Globe theaters had an open space in front called "the pit" or "the yard" (a dirt floor) where people could stand and watch for the admission price of a penny. These people who couldn't afford one of the seats in the upper levels were known as the "groundlings." They might be packed in and uncomfortable, and under an open roof they might have to stand in the rain, but their reactions so close to the stage were excellent for determining what worked with an entire audience, not just the swells in the upper (covered) levels. Isn't it interesting how that's reversed today, with the closest seats being the most expensive of all?

Despite Shakespeare's cultural influence down through the centuries, both during his time and now, people have debated how this "upstart crow" from the small village of Stratford-on-Avon could have possibly been such a literary phenomenon. Thankfully, the 2004 English miniseries "In Search of Shakespeare" written by Michael Wood did very well at showing the Bard's background and actual history, to show how that country boy's skills were developed. And, the show spoke well of his character.

Nevertheless, people will probably continue coming out with books describing who "really" wrote those plays and why the speculators are certain that they are correct. Barring video taken via a time machine that can be believed as not manipulated, the Shakespeare guessing game is just the way of the world. There is how it really is, the speculation otherwise, and how each individual person perceives it to be.

In summary, here's the whole point of the Character part of the Destiny Re-Do formula. You can track back the Habits that led to your Character, but it could be your *perceived* character that led to the Fate you're trying to figure out. You can track back from Habits to Actions to Words to Thoughts. You might not need to consider anyone else in doing that.

When you get to Character, though, you might have been perfect all the way along in achieving your plan, only to end up in an expected Fate due to the perceptions and resultant actions of others. You see this all the time in Hallmark movies, if you watch them. These romance movies almost without fail follow the same formula.

1. Ambitious professional woman goes to her hometown or another small town.
2. She meets her old love who stayed there, or she meets a local

and they clash.

3. They end up teaming together to solve a local problem.
4. They finally fall for each other, then there is a misunderstanding.
5. The ambitious professional woman decides to go back to her other life.
6. In the nick of time, she learns she had a misunderstanding about her guy.
7. They get back together, apologies occur, love blooms.

This formula was used in the very popular Reese Witherspoon movie *Sweet Home Alabama*. People seem to never tire of it. Maybe that's because so many people have had to deal with situations where their character and intentions were misunderstood, or they did the same with others. Call me an optimist – just call me. I like to believe people would rather get along and be happy, than not.

I hope this short dissertation on character and perception of same is helpful to you. It makes me wonder if many of the adverse but character-shaping experiences I have lived through had something to do with eventually writing this book and being more helpful to others.

If so, that's a fate I'm happy with. Next, we'll dive into the last step of the formula. What's your fate? How did you get there? What can you do to make it more enjoyable? I'll do my best to help you sort that out.

Step Six:
Fate Doesn't Have to be Final

THE LAST STEP OF MY formula is not about destiny. That word to me denotes predestination, something planned out for your life but not by you, and such a concept negates the exercise of free will. In my view, the word fate is localized, a particular moment in time. A crossroads you've arrived at, perhaps. That's what I deal with.

Nevertheless, I like moments that feel fated, as though I've stepped into some kind of blessing. I think of that time at age seven when I stopped before crossing a street in my small Texas town, watching falling autumn leaves swirling, magically suspended in the air by a burst of wind. That moment added a mystical feel to my life that would recur many times. I think of being part of a golf team that won a state championship for the small town where I graduated high school. It was the first time anything like that had happened in tiny Anna, Texas (pop. 753 said the town sign). Milling with the crowd in Austin after we received our medals was something special.

Some fated moments were a natural consequence, like the birth of each of my children as I stood by my wife as a birth coach. Others were unexpected and seemed blessed by Heaven, like when I met my wife in a New York theater; time seemed to measurably slow down when she walked in the door. Not long after that, she told me over the phone she thought she'd been married to a famous author in another life, leaving me speechless. I'd been that author, searching in this life for a love from a former life for 16 years. I'd given up the quest to concentrate on my career. Then...boom! I have lived many mystic moments.

I wrote about these things for a year in my Substack called "Chasing Mark Twain" and turned it into a book of the same name. Take a look at skippress.substack.com.

My great times are not the focus of this book. I'm writing this one to help people isolate troubling instances where they feel stuck, or at a crossroads not knowing where to turn. I call this book Destiny Re-Do because I feel that no matter what misfortune you've had so far in life, you can change your destiny going forward with this tool I've been blessed to discover and use.

I work on a single Fate, the present place arrived at, one puzzle at a time. We can't go back and relive portions of our life, but we can gain understanding of how we arrived at certain junctures and work out how to erase wrong patterns so as not to repeat them again.

What is your ultimate destiny? You might have an idea, or you might not. I have a general idea about mine, but I've found that letting my life pleasantly unfold is the best idea. Other than that. I meditate about times to come and try to live as if they are already happening. Meanwhile, with my formula I can isolate and dislodge the results of a bothersome pattern, all the way back to the very thought where it might have begun.

Conversely, once I've dealt with any particular problem – a Fate – I can then use the same structure to work out a plan going forward in the same area of life that I've just straightened out. I don't consider that any time I use the formula it will be a permanent fix, however. Life is constantly in flux. I've done a Destiny Re-Do on other aspects of things I'd previously felt were handled. For instance, one on personal finances might lead to another on money and relationships. Or even, on getting in good physical shape.

When I used the formula and two days later ended up with an extra $30,000 in the bank, based on something I thought about only after gaining a clearer view of my financial situation, that's when I knew I had to share my formula with anyone who could benefit from it.

I've found that people from any strata of society can have the same problems as those of another class. This is because I've written numerous celebrity books, small and large, most prominent being the memoir of superstar singer of the 1950s and 1960s, Patti Page. I've noted patterns in rich people's lives that match the natural ups and downs of poor country people I grew up around in Texas. As such, wealth and fame never meant much to me. My involvement in Hollywood was only a means to and end of being more able to contribute to society.

Maybe that's why I would sometimes get close to celebrity recognition but never crossed the finish line. I simply enjoyed being in the arena. Just prior to meeting the mother of my children, I thought I was going to be a music and movie star, playing Harry Chapin, famous for hits like "Cats in the Cradle" in a movie of his life. The producer of the movie told me I had the part the same night in New York City I by "chance" met the lady I married.

In the process of pursuing that role, I met Harry's hero, Pete Seeger, who was on a musical tour with Arlo Guthrie, who was most famous for "Alice's Restaurant" – the song and movie. After meeting Arlo, I got a great idea for a sequel to that film and went to meet with him at his farm near Stockbridge, Massachusetts to discuss it. He was very interested.

Neither of those movies ended up happening, but I stayed in touch with Arlo and, once I'd written Patti Page's book, I suggested he let me help write his biography. In his quick-witted quirky way, Arlo quipped: "Can't. I don't know how it ends yet."

Similarly, an entertainment attorney of mine was Ringo Starr's best friend. I would try to get him to introduce me to Ringo to talk about writing Ringo's bio, and Bruce would say "Ringo doesn't remember a lot." Finally, Ringo came out with "Photograph" his biography filled with pictures he'd taken over the years. His pictures told his story. Clever, and with the same title of one of his major hits.

It wasn't my destiny to write books with either of those guys, but in recalling each of the stories and mentally running the events through the filter of my formula, I think maybe I could have made at least one of them work. Only, I didn't know the formula then.

How many times have you thought of what might have been? The good thing is, I feel that by using my formula, you might be able to revert some of your own failed ambitions into fulfilled dreams. If you have trouble sorting it all out after reading this book and trying out the formula, you can always try contacting me. As long as I'm still walking the planet, I'll help if I can.

I once interviewed comedian Bob Hope and put him on the cover of a magazine I was editing. Later, I met people who worked with him, and one of the funniest remarks I ever heard came from one of his writers. Asked if he'd been writing all his life, the guy said: "Not yet."

I've found that repeated use of my Destiny Re-Do formula removes wondering about various paths I've taken in life. I get more and more rooted in the present, which sages will tell you is the only thing that exists, anyway. It's all only the present. We can't change our past, but we can change how we feel about it, and get released from any negative hold it has on us. Then, going forward, we have a much better chance of being happy with the unfolding events of our life, day by day.

We can also go forward through the formula and plan things, but I developed it to work backward to sort out how things worked out, to understand why, and to understand how things might go better in the future.

Using the formula that way starts with Fate, so where did we get that word, anyway?

You can find many definitions of the word, including something that happens to a person, or a power considered to cause and control all events, but I've in essence covered those. I consider fate to be a natural consequence of events that a person set in motion. As such, barring freak accidents or acts of God, I consider myself responsible for any situation I find myself in.

The word fate comes from Greek mythology. The Fates are often artistically depicted as beautiful maidens, but the original conception of them was as three crones who spun the threads of human destiny (defined as what will happen in the future). This Greek myth is why the word fate is so often considered synonymous with destiny, but I repeat, I'm not using the word fate in that way.

The Fates were Clotho, Lachesis, and Atropos. The Romans believed in the Fates as well, but named them Nona, Decuma, and Morta. Clotho was the one who spun the "thread" of human fate, while Lachesis handed it out, and Atropos cut the thread when it was time for an individual's death. These goddesses of destiny were collectively known as Moirai (meaning "allotted portion"), and responsible for every Greek's birth, future, past, and death. They wove a human's life, span of life, and end of life, and they also controlled the fate of each Greek god.

I don't know about you, but the prospect of my entire life being determined before I arrived by a trio of old women isn't something I would particularly enjoy. If the Fates truly existed and I tried to use my formula to get a better grip on life, what would happen? Would Clotho protest, Lachesis show up and smack me, and Atropos take me out altogether?

No thank you, Greeks. I wasn't even a fraternity member in college.

The Greeks believed that in the afterlife a person was judged not on their deeds, but on how they dealt with life's challenges. Other cultures had similar beliefs, with variations. For example, Lithuanian folklore described seven goddesses.

Call me modern, but I'd rather judge my own deeds and personally adjust my errors so that I deal with my own sweet fate going forward. I don't like the idea of three all-powerful grandmas manipulating my life, and I don't care how good they might look in modern art.

One thing I do agree on regarding this myth is the idea of a thread running through every person's life. I've worked with hundreds of people to get their stories told, and I always find a theme in each life. Often, I discover a person started off envisioning one path for their life that turned into something completely different. For example, my late friend Patti Page originally intended to be a commercial artist. I knew I'd be a writer early on, but I got distracted for years also pursuing music and acting. Still, both Patti and I had an artistic "thread" that we followed.

As you are sorting out the Fate you are currently trying to improve, you might consider the thread or theme of your life. Did you end up where you are due to some endeavor that you thought you should do, instead of what your intuition said you'd be happiest pursuing?

By that last line, I don't suggest someone should concentrate on doing only what they think makes them happy. That can be transitory. People can get confused, thinking that when Joseph Campbell or a life coach says "Follow your bliss" that means dropping responsibilities and only doing things that make you smile. Some people believe they are happy being high all the time, while others relentlessly pursue a hedonistic lifestyle. I've known too many people like that, and I could never consider any of them happy. An entire society constantly living for thrills would become a total disaster.

I've always supported myself as an adult and have been lucky enough to find ways to keep the bills paid. Responsibility is one thing that makes me happy, and being responsible got a major boost after one session of my Destiny Re-Do formula.

So, do you wonder how to dissect the current Fate you're struggling with?

I find it helps to write it out so that you become exterior to it, so it's not in your head but in front of your eyes. People who write honest memoirs and biographies gain insight this way.

There were times in my life that I dearly wish I'd known about the approach I've developed, because putting my considerations on paper would have helped clarify my thoughts and prevented me from major mistakes.

One of my mistakes turned out tragically. When I was in my 30s, years before I met the woman I married, I was tired of not being happily coupled. It occurred to me that I might be missing something in my approach. I decided to find out if what my dates were looking for in a mate matched what I assumed they wanted. Then I reasoned the single women I met were not successful as far as being part of a happy couple. Why not ask women who had achieved happy coupling? I made a list of admirable women I knew who were attached or married and I contacted them to see if those women knew something the single women did not know.

I made interesting discoveries, such as hearing from a famous actress who told me that when she met her husband, he wasn't making much money, but she saw potential in him, and his other qualities made up for lack of finances. That shot down a fixed idea of mine that I would have to be rich to make a relationship with someone like that work. I thought of a famous soap opera actress I'd been set up with who lived in a luxury condo and owned a Bentley. I felt inadequate but never bothered to discuss lifestyles with her, so we never had a second date.

I had also not pursued other famous and beautiful women I felt "lesser" than.

When I met the lady I married, our lifestyles melded perfectly. During my "ask the successful women" venture, though, I found that one woman I thought was engaged had broken the engagement. She also was a successful actress but a bit too good at it. I ended up moving in with her and finding out she was a major alcoholic who covered it up very well until a man found out, then the relationship ended. This romantic excursion became a major disaster of my life.

How did I end up at that Fate? By not trusting my intuition and initial Thought that I should find out why she broke up with her fiancé, a guy I knew and respected. I didn't even bother to inquire with him.

I ignored my intuition (Thought), didn't converse (Words), and took the Actions of falling for her looks and sex. I hadn't concentrated on sex; I wanted a mate. I forgot that.

Had I used the Destiny Re-Do back then, as soon as I had doubts about pursuing that relationship, I would have asked myself "What kind of Character would end up in a Fate like this?" The answer would have been "A Character who isn't really trying to find the right mate but has simply fallen for looks and fun and sex, even if she is an alcoholic."

From that point, I would have considered doing similar things in the past (Habit), seen the folly of the Actions that created that Habit, and looked at the Words I'd written describing my ideal partner. The lady I got together with didn't match my Words because I didn't want anyone with major problems – I'd tried too often to "fix" people in the past. She was the last.

There's a personal example from me. For you, it gets down to defining the Fate currently troubling you and then working backward to see what kind of Character would *create* such a Fate. If it's a faulty Character, there is a Habit or Habits that fueled that Character, and then you roll on back to some concept (Thought) that you had about solving a problem in your life.

My friend Daniel Petrie Jr., a successful screenwriter/director, once had an office in the same building as Hollywood legend Billy Wilder, whose "Some Like It Hot" was voted best comedy movie of all-time by the American Film Institute. Dan told me that several times, he'd seen Billy pace the hallway in the "Writer's Building" on Little Santa Monica in Beverly Hills. The third act of Billy's current screenplay wasn't working out right, so he'd pace and think it over.

Inevitably, Dan said, Billy would find the problem in the first act. Then he and his co-writing partner would make adjustments, and the problem in the third act ending would work itself out.

If you have an unfortunate Fate to deal with, somewhere along the line of Thoughts / Words / Actions / Habits you may have gone off the track of your original idea, and in doing so, you got the Fate you ended up with.

In contrast, when you get the sequence right, you end up with a Fate that you love, and it aligns with the original Thought or Thoughts you had that began the whole process. An example is my golf team championship in high school. My buddy and I played a lot of golf and we found that other friends of ours did as well. A cousin of one of our buddies whose dad was a golf pro moved to town and we put together a team. With plenty of practice we all got better, attracted a coach, competed with other schools, won the regional championship, and then won at state.

None of this would have happened if we hadn't pursued the thought that maybe we could finally win a championship for our tiny Texas town.

Once you practice using my formula to sort out situations that trouble you, you might find as I have that you can successfully plan out and execute future endeavors to your satisfaction. To that end, the next chapter is a condensed workshop in repairing an unwanted Fate.

After that, I'll take the same situation and present a scenario of how an original thought can be developed into a major goal and achieved. I've hinted at such a process here, in describing a very bad relationship I had and, chronologically after that, finally finding the mate I'd sought for 16 years. I haven't just made this stuff up – I've lived it.

Keep in mind, if there is any confusion, you can reach me for consultation. I'm glad to help.

Let's get started on your Destiny Re-Do.

Step Seven:
Your Destiny Redone

LOUISE HAY, FOUNDER of Hay House Publishing, had a philosophy. She said: "I do not fix problems. I fix my thinking. Then problems fix themselves." That's what happens using my formula. Among other things, it's a way to track a pattern of behavior that began with a thought and ended up in a situation that is less than optimum.

Louise Hay also said: "Every thought we think is creating our future." I'm not sure I agree with that one because we can have thoughts that pass and *are not acted upon*, but I get her point. Thoughts do lead to words and words to actions, and when mentality results in real world activity, then we're on a path to the future.

So, here's a thought. Let's run through the procedure of Destiny Re-Do. I assume you might like that, as long as I haven't bored you so far.

1. Backtrack from Fate. That is, the current situation, the moment in time where you've reached an uncomfortable or even intolerable situation. You need to clearly describe it, as specifically as possible, so you fully understand it. When it's out of your head and written out, you can confront it more easily and see it clearly.

2. What Character Got You There? There's an old Chinese saying that when you get old, you get the face you deserve. The Bible says you reap (harvest) what you sow (plant). The phrase that started me on the path with this formula was the idea that Character determines Destiny. Thus, once I've understood the current circumstances I'm in, which I call a Fate, I immediately ask what kind of Character would elicit the present situation.

3. What Habit or Habits Led to that Character? Just to make it simple, I'll be very graphic. Someone gets on drugs and stays there. It's a habit; let's say it's heroin. That character is referred to as "junkie." (A slang term for heroin is "junk.") The Destiny that often follows being a junkie is death. Or, someone could have a gambling habit and become a compulsive gambler, and their Fate could be "broke." On a calmer note, when I used the formula to deal with recurring lean financial times, I determined that the Character I ended up with was a mentality of thinking *there was nothing I could do about it.* Which was a lie because I *always* did something to revert tough money situations. In short, I got into a Habit of being a Character feeling defeated and it was an attitude I bought into as a small child when I wanted to help the family but was told I could not.

4. What Actions Created that Habit or Habits? This is where self-examination may take a while. Habits are created when actions are repeated, and both the actions and habits can be good or bad. If you're trying to revert an unwanted fate, once you isolate the habit that put you in that situation, you'll likely end up reviewing a pattern of actions that resulted in the habit, and finally get down to the action you took that started you on the road to the problem you're now trying to handle. Let's say your fate was ending up in a terrible relationship. The action of beginning the relationship might be the root of the problem, but that's not as likely as ignoring those "red flags" the way people do when enthralled by emotions and hormones in the beginning of a romance. Whatever the situation is, I advise writing down the actions or even one action, if that's all it took. It's like creating a backward road map to understand exactly where you came from to get where you are; The good thing is, once you've been through the process a few times, it gets much easier to use.

5. Do You Remember the Words? If you're faced with the possible breakup of a marriage, the wedding service where you said "I do" is probably not where the trouble started. A common situation is ignoring red flags – in a relationship, on a job, or elsewhere. As mentioned earlier, non-action can be an action; that is, something with consequences. Perhaps you're hired to do a certain job for which you're eminently qualified. Communication is great until you're given a task to do that you know nothing about. You convey your concern, but it's brushed off. You drop it, but your boss takes your acquiescence as a sign that you can be manipulated, and you won't stand your ground. That starts a pattern that ends up in you quitting at a financially inopportune time because you can't take the mistreatment anymore. What if you'd spoken up and insisted on better treatment? Maybe you'd have been fired, but you'd probably have had a better fate, because who wants to work in an oppressive environment?

6. Did You Effectively Think Things Through? Once more, I am reminded of how Nikola Tesla would completely construct a new invention in his mind before he ever sketched it out or tried to build it. Not many people have that kind of focus, but you can also think something to death without a conclusion, and never get into action. Here's an example I've run into repeatedly in my life. People come to me who always wanted to write but they never put words on paper on a regular basis, never developed a habit of continually improving their work, thus never adopting the persona of being a writer. Then, maybe after retiring from a different career, they decide to do something they always wanted to do – write a book and get it published. I've taught, counseled, and edited hundreds of people like that. I don't admire the fate they ended up with, but I don't mention that. I just give them the tools and counseling they need to finally get published.

I'll give you a real-life example of how the formula worked for someone I knew. I was once roommates with another writer with whom I sold a screenplay. Let's call him Sean. After I moved out, he got a larger place and for a roommate he took in a young writer we'd known since the kid was a teenager. I'll call that one John. New roommate John turned out to have amazing talent as a screenwriter and got a lot of notice in Hollywood. My former roommate Sean supported John while John wrote a script that put him on the Hollywood talent map. When the movie was made, it ended up with Academy Awards.

Naturally, my friend Sean lost his roommate, but they stayed friends. John began directing movies he wrote and did well. Then Sean had a thought. He needed a business loan.

Sean Thoughts – *Maybe he'll co-sign the loan for me. After all, I supported him and never asked him to pay me back.*

Words – John, who was by now a Hollywood celebrity, had many people asking him for money and he was also about to get a divorce. So, he wouldn't co-sign a loan for Sean. They had "words" and it looked like the friendship was over.

Actions – Sean got a loan, anyway. Writer/director John got a divorce. Sean began writing a book that would eventually get published and earn him good money. Meanwhile, I had a family and wasn't much in touch with either of them.

Habits – Basically, both friends just continued with their lives and though Sean made a few attempts to reconcile, busy Hollywood guy John just kept living his life.

Character – Sean gave up on trying to fix the friendship but brought it up to me one day when I asked if anything had changed. It hadn't. Sean still deeply wished to repair the situation.

Fate – I don't like to see people estranged from each other, particularly over something that seems trivial. So, I resolved to do something if I could, but I didn't have a plan.

That put me at a *Thought* of "Let's see if this can be fixed." I didn't feel like my contacting John about the situation would work, so I let it rest. Instead, I gave Sean a tool I thought would help him. I told him about the Hawaiian practice of h'onoponopono, the four-step process of apologizing for something, asking forgiveness, saying thank you, then adding "I love you."

More on that later, but I told Sean to work it on himself over letting the loss of friendship affect him so deeply. He needed to love himself, release the bad emotions, and accept whatever might happen. He tried it and handled his side of the problem, amazed how much relief he got.

Then by "chance" (which I believe in less the longer I live), I got an invitation to a screening of John's new movie from a company promoting it. I saw there would be a Q&A after the showing, and that was an opportunity. I went and sat in the front row. Now my thought plan that something could be done had a chance, or was at least worth a try.

When the Q&A was over, I spoke with John and told him how proud I was of him, now an A-list Hollywood writer/director. What a long way it had been from when he was a poor teenager. Prior to speaking with John, I thought he might not want to hear about Sean if I mentioned him, but instead, John was friendly and didn't flinch when I mentioned Sean. Time healed wounds, I surmised. We had a pleasant few moments catching up.

The next day, I contacted Sean and discussed what happened. I said I told John that I'd invited Sean to the screening, but he couldn't get out of another commitment.

I inherently knew that my two friends had a misunderstanding about intentions. My former roommate Sean had thought it was no big deal to ask our rich friend John to cosign a loan, given that Sean had supported John a long time when John wrote the hit screenplay. I imagined that John, being in the middle of a divorce and being hit on for money from other people, hadn't thought things through and Sean wanting a loan co-signer was just another big irritation.

So, there were words, then actions (estrangement) and the estrangement became a habit. Each of my friends misinterpreted the other's character, and their fate was sealed as a former friendship.

After hearing about how good the movie was and John's benign reaction to hearing Sean's name, my former roommate wondered how he should get in touch. I suggested he send John an email (that he could answer at his leisure), say that I said I'd loved John's movie, and to congratulate our friend on its success. No mention of any of the unfortunate past circumstances.

Why that suggestion? Because they'd gone off the track with *words*. My friend who had maintained the upset the most (Sean) got over the emotions with the h'onoponopono practice, so now he was in the good frame of mind he'd been in *before* their upset.

That worked. John replied quickly and suggested they get together when he got back from filming his new movie in England. A friendship break of several years had been resolved.

The catch was this. As I had learned from using the h'onoponopono method, as I had learned using the Yuen Method, when a person changes internally, the world will usually change as well, mirror-like, to the point it often seems like magic.

Sean resolved the emotions of his upset and removed a barrier to handing the problem. Because I understand the steps of my formula, I figured out the point at which the friendship went off the rails. I then thought it through effectively, picked the right words and actions to get things resolved, and the solution arrived.

When using my formula, I always start with the Fate that someone is concerned with. Then I start backtracking to find out where things went wrong – it can be at *any* of the steps. I've done the formula on myself often, and one of the times discovered that a pattern started off with wrong thinking on my part. Other times it was wrong actions, like not getting enough training to enable me to succeed in some goal I was pursuing.

The part of the formula that is inflexible is that the sequence is always there: thoughts to words to actions to habits to character to destiny/fate.

If you'd like to know more about h'onoponopono, study https://hooponoponomiracle.com and read about Morrnah Nalamaku Simeona, a Hawaiian Kahuna. She founded the modern-day ho'oponopono. As the site says, "it's all about healing yourself, releasing your limitations and negativity, and becoming free." And it works!

I hope by now you feel comfortable using my back-engineering of a famous old phrase to fix small and large problems. Like Louise Hay, I have the approach of fixing my thinking and letting problems then get fixed on their own.

Ultimately, your destiny is your doing, particularly if, like me, you believe you can take charge of your life at any point and improve it. I hope my formula helps you and, once again, you're welcome to get in touch with me any time you'd like to discuss it.

There's one more thing. Once a problem's been straightened out, why not develop a plan to achieve the goal you originally wanted?

That's right – the formula works both backward and forward! I cover that in the next chapter.

Bonus Round:
Planning a Destiny

WITH A DESTINY RE-DO, you start with the end result (which I call a Fate for reasons stated), and then you study back down the other steps, to find out where and how things went wrong.

When you're making an action plan to accomplish something, you have the end result in mind. Therefore, you start with a goal. When I'm doing that, I thoroughly massage that thought mentally. Maybe I don't try to build an electric motor in my mind like Nikola Tesla did, but I envision my goal as perfectly as I can imagine.

Then I write it out and adjust and edit the statement until I'm happy with it. When I've described my goal satisfactorily, I print it out and put it in a prominent place so if I choose, I can recite it out loud every day. (And I try to do that at least on a regular basis.)

Repetition can work wonders. I discovered that when I advise writers to map out scheduled times in their life when they plan to write, and they allow no one to interrupt unless there is an emergency, that arrangement fuels their ambitions, because they've built a secure space in their life to pursue an often heart-felt ambition.

Lifestyle gurus will tell you to treat a goal as if you have already achieved it. Act like you're already living it. I've experienced that often. When I'm a positive mood and happy, I feel lucky, and I find that's when I win money with scratch-off tickets or in contests. I don't consider myself a gambler, never play poker or go to Las Vegas, but I've learned a lot about improving my intuition by testing with small ticket bets.

You may have felt as I have that everyone on Earth is a bit like a personal radio station. The signals we send out are easily received, and when others like our transmissions, they express it. In scientific terms, happiness is a higher wavelength, and it's certainly possible to make yourself happy. It can appear that having enough money can make someone happy, but the truth is, having enough money to feel secure in life going forward is more like the ticket we want.

It's usually security that we seek. Just watch some happy children playing, knowing they have stability and protection with parents or caregivers. It's the same thing with older people in retirement homes. If you've ever rescued a sad dog from the pound, you've likely seen a dramatic personality change once they fully realize they've been rescued.

My use of the formula in this book repeatedly makes me more secure in my life. When I honestly examine how things went awry in my life on any given subject, I have much more confidence going forward. By taking full responsibility for everything in my life, I am made stronger.

When a person has that kind of attitude, they have less doubts about the actions they take. Accordingly, I've turned actions into good habits that have done well for me, from dieting to exercise, to my writing, to mental and spiritual improvement.

When I use these steps consciously and positively, I exhibit good character and am happier with myself. As such, I consider it inevitable that I will achieve any goal I conceive, as long as I adjust when necessary and stick with my plan.

Sometimes, I'll even meditate on what kind of character I would be to feel secure about the possibilities of achieving a persona goal. I repeatedly relied on role models as a poor kid in Texas. I read about real-life heroes and watched them in movies and on TV. I'm far from along in that. How many times have you seen a sports champion on television talking about admiring and emulating a champion they watched as a youth? That shows how important it is for people to have heroes and good examples to emulate.

Keep that in mind when you achieve a great goal – be a good example.

Some people who never participated much in organized sports think that great ability demonstrated is something you're simply born with. The truth is, great champions often simply work harder at it than others. They have a habit of thousands of repetitions to improve their skills, so it looks effortless when they're playing their game. They figure out what works and what doesn't work and they persit until they perfect their skills.

Conversely, people who reach an elevated state of existence – like becoming a celebrity, or winning a championship, or getting a windfall of money – who do not have a life balanced and grounded, very often make a mess of things. I don't have to give you any of those examples. Unless you've been living in a cave, you've seen them constantly in the media.

Here's one more thing that I've noticed in my many years. When you are secure enough in the idea of something great that you want to achieve, you will not give up on its accomplishment no matter what. I've seen this over and over in the arts. It took Sir Richard Attenborough 25 years to get the movie "Gandhi" made – he never gave up. J.K. Rowling got turned down 12 times with Harry Potter before getting published. George Lucas got turned down with "Star Wars."

I feel, based on my own experience and how I've helped others, that once you use this Destiny Re-Do formula to unravel a problem that's bothering you and then you do the steps in forward motion, beginning with thoroughly envisioned thoughts, you have a much higher possibility of success. Still, *life is not a drive-through route to fame and fortune*! You must persist with confidence and determination, believing in yourself and the integrity of your vision. The hardest-won prize is often the most valued.

I've helped perhaps half a million people become better writers with my books and courses. I got the most satisfaction from those who become published and sold. Similarly, when I help someone sort out a life problem and see the smile on their face and hear the enthusiasm in their voice, there is nothing better.

I wish you all the best in great achievements and am always happy to help. After using my formula to fix a problem, if you're still interested in the same goal you were stopped from achieving, try the steps going forward to form your battle plan and *keep working that plan*!

I know you can achieve your goals, even your "impossible" ones, because I did.

Best of luck to you, and may your destiny come out exactly the way that you imagine it will! Now, here's...

To Your New Beginning!

Don't miss out!

Visit the website below and you can sign up to receive emails whenever Skip Press publishes a new book. There's no charge and no obligation.

https://books2read.com/r/B-A-TMEJ-MNWBD

BOOKS 2 READ

Connecting independent readers to independent writers.

Did you love *Destiny Re-Do*? Then you should read *Screenplay to Novel: Real Money from Used Pages*[4] by Skip Press!

5

A ten-step guide to turning any screenplay into an excellent novel that you can sell, whether the script sold or not, by the author of the *Complete Idiot's Guide to Screenwritng*, who has had more than 50 books and novels published and taught 100,000+ writers to be more profitable.

Read more at www.skippress.com.

---

4. https://books2read.com/u/4Ax2gN

5. https://books2read.com/u/4Ax2gN

Also by Skip Press

Screenplay to Novel: Real Money from Used Pages
Destiny Re-Do

Watch for more at www.skippress.com.

About the Author

I've written, produced and directed plays, edited a Hollywood entertainment magazine, made instructional videos, sold screenplays, served as Hollywood reporter for magazines, been a staff writer for a United Paramount Network kids show, published young adult novels and non–fiction, and taught an online screenwriting course that was available in 1,500 schools. I've had books published both under my name and as a ghostwriter, including the Complete Idiot's Guide to Screenwriting and How To Write What You Want & Sell What You Write.I helped start the Hollywood Film Festival and wrote This Is My Song: A Memoir, by music legend Patti Page with Skip Press.

Check my portfolio at - https://www.pinterest.com/skippress/
Read more at www.skippress.com.